CHARLES HARRIS

Radiant BOOKS

Gospel Publishing House/Springfield, Mo. 65802

02-0897

Library of Congress Catalog Card Number 80-84173
International Standard Book Number 0-88243-897-2
Printed in the United States of America

A teacher's guide for individual or group study with this book is available from the Gospel Publishing House.

Contents

1   The Future Is Certain   5

2   The Trip of a Lifetime!   15

3   A Terrible Time Ahead   25

4   The Man of Deception   35

5   A Reign of Terror   45

6   Choosing the Right Side   55

7   He's Coming Again!   64

8   Israel—Going Home Again   73

9   Christ's Rule of Righteousness   82

10   The World to Come   91

11   What Happens When a
        Person Dies?   100

12   The Court of No Appeal   109

13   Time Without End   119

1

The Future Is Certain

REVELATION 1:12-18; 19:10

Natural Curiosity

On the night former President Nixon returned to America from his historic trip to China, a young man was a bit late returning home from collecting on his paper route. As the boy rushed into the living room of his home, he asked breathlessly, "Is he back yet? Did anything go wrong?"

The lad was aware that a well-known psychic had predicted a catastrophe in connection with the president's travels to the Far East. When his parents informed him that the trip had ended and all was well, the youth seemed a bit surprised. Like most people, he was curious about the prophecies of those who claim insight into the future.

Natural curiosity is harmless, and sometimes can be most helpful. It has led many inquiring persons to discoveries that have considerably relieved mankind's miseries. However, when it comes to delving into the future apart from God, Scripture condemns such curiosity as sinful.

In the Old Testament, the Lord repeatedly told His people not to consult fortune-tellers and the like. He said there should not be among them "any one that... useth divination, or an observer of times, or an enchanter, or a witch, or a charmer, or a consulter with familiar spirits, or a wizard, or a necromancer" (Deuteronomy 18:10,11).

It seems clear enough, then, that God does not want His people to practice spiritism, to attend seances and try to communicate with the dead, or to consult the horoscope in the daily newspaper. Instead, Isaiah says, they should commit their future to the Lord. He declares: "And when they shall say unto you, Seek unto them that have familiar spirits, and unto wizards that peep and that mutter: should not a people seek unto their God?" (Isaiah 8:19).

Spiritual Hunger

But even when a person comes to the Lord concerning the future, he must watch his motives. Prophecy was not placed in the Bible to appeal to man's curiosity. The thing God denies us in turning to fortune-tellers He does not permit in coming to Him. The disciples asked Jesus about the future with an unacceptable motive. His reply was: "It is not for you to know the times or the seasons, which the Father hath put in his own power" (Acts 1:7).

Yet, someone has calculated that over 1,000 passages in the Bible were written initially as prophecy. They total from one-fourth to one-half of the entire Book. Many of them have already been literally fulfilled precisely as predicted.

If not to satisfy curiosity, then, what is the purpose of prophecy in Scripture? The Lord's intent in sharing some things about tomorrow with His people is to point men to Jesus as the One who is in control of the future.

God provided two tests for the prophet of Old Testament times. Whether or not his prediction came true was one way to tell if he was genuine (Deuteronomy 18:20-22). However, even if his word came true, men were warned not to follow a prophet whose purpose was to turn their hearts from Jehovah (Deuteronomy 13:1-3).

Those with hungry hearts who seek to draw closer to God through a study of Biblical prophecy will find that the future is theirs in Jesus. But those with different motives will find only confusion.

The Bible student will not find minute details concerning every aspect of the future in Scripture. However, he will find that a study of prophecy reinforces his confidence in the Bible, has a positive effect on his daily life, and enriches his worship of Jesus.

Predictive Ability

One of the reasons for concluding that the Bible is inspired by God is its predictive ability. Its Author told Abram his descendants would remain in Egypt a minimum of 400 years (Genesis 15:13). Their exodus from bondage came after 430 years in Egypt as predicted (Exodus 12:41). The God who knows and controls tomorrow is worthy of trust. The Book in which He reveals some of His great knowledge can be read with confidence.

One of the differences between what Jehovah said in the Old Testament and the voices of false gods was their lack of ability to foretell the future. Through Isaiah, God chided the idols for their weakness:

> Let them bring forth, and show us what shall happen: let them show the former things, what they

be, that we may consider them, and know the latter end of them; or declare us things for to come. Show the things that are to come hereafter, that we may know that ye are gods (Isaiah 41:22,23).

In the same way, a basic difference between the Bible and other sacred books, such as the Koran of the Moslems or the Vedas of the Hindus, is that they have little or no predictive prophecy, while the Bible has an abundance of it. Many passages, chapters, and even whole Books of the Bible (16 Old Testament Books and one New Testament Book) are devoted to the subject of prophecy. Some of it has been fulfilled, some of it is being fulfilled, and all of it will ultimately be fulfilled.

By the revelation of God, Joseph predicted the 7 years of plenty followed by 7 years of famine in Egypt (Genesis 41:25-32). Both came exactly as he had said.

With insight provided by the Spirit of the Lord, Daniel spoke years in advance of the fall of Babylon to Medo-Persia (Daniel 2:36-39; 8:20). His prophecy became history in 536 B.C. He also told of the breakup of Greece into four divisions (Daniel 8:21,22). His words were fulfilled following the death of Alexander the Great in 332 B.C.

Some 40 years before it happened, Jesus foretold the fall of Jerusalem to the Romans (Luke 21:20-24). His teachings on the tragedy include at least two dozen details of the event. All were fulfilled to the letter when Titus and the Roman legions took the city in A.D. 70.

Fulfilled prophecy proves the reliability of God's Word. As Jesus said: "And now I have told you before it come to pass, that, when it is come to pass, ye might believe" (John 14:29).

Practical Prophecy

But of what practical value is prophecy? One young lady declared she felt like curling up in the pew and going to sleep every time she heard her pastor say his subject for a service was prophecy. Why spend time on something that some feel has no direct bearing on one's life? The truth is God intended prophecy to have a decided effect on the daily life of the individual.

One item in keeping with this purpose of prophecy is that it promotes an overcoming Christian life. A study of eschatology, the doctrine of last things, has a sanctifying effect on the serious student of Scripture. John speaks about pondering the truths of Christ's second coming. He concludes: "And every man that hath this hope in him purifieth himself, even as he is pure" (1 John 3:3).

The practical purpose of prophecy is also revealed in the fact that it provokes prayer. Daniel "understood by books the number of the years" the Babylonian captivity of Israel would last (Daniel 9:2). When he calculated by the calendar that the 70 years predicted by Jeremiah were near an end, he went to earnest prayer about the matter.

Prophecy does not lead one to a fatalistic resignation that "whatever will be, will be." Rather, it tells the person how he may joyously cooperate in God's plan for the ages. Herein, in a sense at least, is the forecasting of the believer's future.

Further, general information about what is ahead serves to strengthen and encourage God's people. If He tells them beforehand that the going might get rough, that fact helps them hold steady, knowing the Lord is in control of everything, regardless of what happens.

Jesus had this in mind when He said: "And when ye shall hear of wars and rumors of wars, be ye not troubled: for such things must needs be" (Mark 13:7). Jesus meant that His people should be comforted rather than terrified by the teachings of prophecy.

All of the Bible's prophecy is much like the Book of Revelation. As mysterious as the Book seems to some, it has great practical value. Anyone who reads it is guaranteed a blessing by Jesus himself (Revelation 1:3). It is not necessary to understand every little detail of the Book to receive this promised benefit.

Besides, the Christian is to "keep those things which are written therein" (Revelation 1:3). There is much in Revelation that is understandable and applicable to one's daily life. This is true of all Biblical prophecy.

Prophetic Experts

But some may say, "Which prophetic expert am I to follow? None of them seem to agree." One pastor declared he had heard so many differing opinions on what the Bible says about the future that he shunned them all. By neglecting this important segment of God's Word in his preaching, he left his congregation lacking in the guidance God intended them to have. One need not be a specialist to share simple truths of Scripture on the subject of prophecy.

Instructions from the Bible about tomorrow are necessary to steer the Christian away from the frightening proclamations of false teachers about prophecy. Warning that false christs and false teachers would arise to lead people astray, Jesus said: "Behold, I have told you before" (Matthew 24:25).

At Thessalonica, some were saying the severe persecution of the first century meant the Christians were living in the Tribulation period of prophecy. This teaching was extremely upsetting to the young converts in the infant church, who expected to be spared from the Tribulation. Paul wrote to correct the error. He assured them they were not then experiencing, nor would they ever experience, the Great Tribulation. He concluded by saying: "Remember ye not, that , when I was with you, I told you these things?" (2 Thessalonians 2:5).

Then there were misunderstandings at Thessalonica about life after death. Some expected Jesus to return so soon that they thought those who died before the event had failed in their faith. Paul assured them that those alive in Christ at the Second Coming would have no advantage over those who had died in Jesus. His final exhortation was: "Comfort one another with these words" (1 Thessalonians 4:18).

Speculation Versus Worship

The purpose of prophecy is to promote worship of Jesus, not useless speculation about the future. In fact, the bulk of Biblical prophecy centers on Christ. It is estimated that more than 300 details concerning His first coming to earth were foretold. Each prediction was fulfilled to the letter.

Even in Genesis, the first Book of the Bible, prophetic information pointed men to the Saviour who would come. No sooner had man sinned than God promised salvation.

11

In one short verse the basic events of the life of Jesus were foretold (Genesis 3:15). This passage gives a prophetic glimpse of the virgin birth of God's Son as the "seed of woman." Certainly, the Incarnation is referred to here, and the verse speaks of Christ's death as an occasion where Satan would "bruise his heel." But, Genesis 3:15 also looks forward to the victory of Jesus over the devil at the cross. In the end, God promised the seed of woman would bruise the head of Satan.

Prophetic passages in the middle of the Bible also point men to Jesus. His virgin birth is clearly predicted (Isaiah 7:14). Micah reveals even the exact place of His birth (Micah 5:2). The small town of Bethlehem in Judea would welcome Him into the world. David tells of His death, burial, and resurrection (Psalm 16:10).

Toward the end of the Bible, prophecy again is a source of encouragement to the worship of Jesus. After having general events of the future revealed to him by an angel, John was ready to fall down before the heavenly messenger. But the angel stopped him and said: "Worship God: for the testimony of Jesus is the spirit of prophecy" (Revelation 19:10).

Granted, a person could spend his time in prophetic ponderings to little profit. He might be somewhat terrified with thoughts that he had knowledge of some unpleasant event of the future over which he had no control.

But if the believer uses the study of the prophetic portions of God's Word as a means of drawing closer to the Lord, things will be different. No, he will not find a forecast of his own personal future in Scripture. Predicting individual fortunes does not promote the commitment of one's tomorrow to the Lord. Rather, the Christian will, through prophecy, hear Jesus saying as He did in a lesson on the subject long ago: "Watch, take heed, pray, and see that you not be troubled" (Mark 13:5,7,9,23, 33,35, paraphrased).

Prayerful Humility

The prophetic teachings of the Bible are of such a nature that prayerful humility is necessary in approaching the subject. One always needs the help of the Lord in studying the Bible. As Paul says:

> But the natural man receiveth not the things of the Spirit of God: for they are foolishness unto him: neither can he know them, because they are spiritually discerned (1 Corinthians 2:14).

But this is especially true with regard to the Bible's prophecy. Some of it is in symbolic language and requires careful study.

The wisdom of the Lord is manifested in the way He presents His message of tomorrow. While the general outline is plain enough, God has not given so many minute details of the future that a mastery of prophecy makes one an expert to be revered by his fellowmen.

Some teachers regard themselves as so knowledgeable in the subject that they appear to brag about their insights into the future. They sometimes seem to say, "Ask me anything about what's ahead. I have all the answers." One went so far as to say he had been making predictions about soon-coming events in the world for 35 years and had never been wrong!

Biblical teachings about tomorrow were not intended to boost such sinful pride of man. They were not meant as a means of drawing undue attention to the preacher of prophecy. The Lord has all things arranged so "no flesh should glory in his presence" (1 Corinthians 1:29).

Even prophets like Daniel didn't know everything about the future. In fact, he didn't understand some of the things he wrote. When he asked for enlightenment, he was told, in essence, that some prophecy is understood best only near the time of its fulfillment (Daniel 12:4,8,9).

Strangely enough, it was not until after they were fulfilled that some of Jesus' prophetic declarations were understood by His disciples. His teachings about His own resurrection are among the most notable (Luke 18:31-34; John 12:16).

Those who failed to see Jesus as the predicted Messiah knew a lot of Old Testament prophecy. They even knew the exact place of His birth (Matthew 2:4-6). But they overlooked other teachings of Scripture, such as those referring to Christ's suffering. Therefore, they failed to recognize Him when He came.

Seeing the shortcomings of others in the study of prophecy suggests that today's student should seek God's help in his efforts. His main motive should be to personally profit and to glorify God. To desire understanding of what the Bible teaches about tomorrow merely for knowledge's sake will not do.

2

The Trip of a Lifetime!

1 THESSALONIANS 4:13-18

Ready, Set, Go!

The big church bus rolls along its prescribed route every Sunday morning. Its red, white, and blue colors suggest not so much a patriotic theme as theological truths: The hearts of sinful men can be cleansed (made *white*) by the blood of Jesus Christ (*red*). Then they will be ready for heaven beyond the skies of *blue*.

An interesting slogan also appears in large letters on each side of the church bus: "One shall be taken, and the other left behind." No doubt the immediate intent of these words is to encourage those who ride the bus to be ready when it stops at their door, or risk not getting to go to Sunday school that day.

However, the slogan also serves a higher purpose. Taken from Matthew 24:40,41, it encourages readiness for a greater journey. The major message of the exhortation is that everyone who reads it should be prepared for the rapture of all living Christians at the second coming of Christ. Going to heaven with Him when He comes for His children will be the trip of a lifetime!

Means of Transportation

Rapture is the word generally used by theologians to speak of this trip that Christians will take through the sky. Like the term *Trinity*, the word itself is not found in Scripture, but the truths it signifies plainly appear on the pages of the Bible.

Originally, rapture was a word that was commonly used without any theological significance. To "rapture" meant simply to carry something from one place to another, or to move it from one location to another. By definition, the word also suggests the idea of seizing or taking hold of an object, with sufficient force to lift it and transfer it to a desired place.

Transportation, then, is the basic idea behind the term *rapture*. This common word was borrowed by the Church and used to speak of the transportation of Christians to heaven without dying.

The Bible gives several plain statements and some pictures as previews of the Rapture. It teaches that the event may occur at any time. Scripture also indicates that the Rapture must be distinguished from the revelation of Christ. Many Bible scholars speak of the two as different phases of the Second Coming, while others prefer to call only the Revelation the Second Coming. Accompanying these truths in the Bible, are numerous exhortations to prepare for the Rapture.

Departure Schedule

Upon considering what Scripture says on the subject, it becomes clear the Rapture is the next thing on God's calendar of future events. From

New Testament times up to the present, Christians have expected the return of Christ at any moment. In theological terms, the second coming of the Lord has always been viewed as imminent.

While discussing His return before He went away, Jesus taught His disciples that His coming would be sudden and unexpected and could occur at any moment. To illustrate His point, the Lord told a story of an estate owner who took a trip for an indefinite period of time. He encouraged his employees to work diligently while he was away. The conclusion of the parable contained the exhortation:

> Watch ye therefore: for ye know not when the master of the house cometh, at even, or at midnight, or at the cockcrowing, or in the morning: lest coming suddenly he find you sleeping (Mark 13:35,36).

Jesus also compared His return to earth to the visit of a thief. Naturally, a burglar does not announce the time of his arrival. The Lord exhorted: "Be ye therefore ready also: for the Son of man cometh in an hour when ye think not" (Luke 12:40).

The writers of the Epistles taught that the return of Jesus was imminent. The author of the Book of Hebrews declared: "For yet a little while, and he that shall come will come, and will not tarry" (Hebrews 10:37). The import of his words in the Greek is that it will be only a very little while.

James declared the coming of the Lord was drawing near (James 5:8). Paul saw the working of the Antichrist, an end-time event, as beginning in his day (2 Thessalonians 2:7). John had reason to think he lived in the last days (1 John 2:18; 4:3).

17

Why the Delay?

Obviously, some 2,000 years have passed since the early Christians expected the Lord to return at any moment. Some people question the correctness of an emphasis on the Biblical passages suggesting the imminence of the Rapture. They focus on Scripture passages that show a lot of work was to be done between the ascension of Christ and His return. The nations needed to be evangelized (Matthew 28:19,20). The world must hear the gospel (Acts 1:5-8). The Kingdom must necessarily fill the hearts of men before it covers the earth under the reign of Jesus during the Millennium (Matthew 13:1-50).

Besides, Peter knew he would live to a ripe old age (John 21:18,19). Paul learned from the Lord that he would have an extensive ministry (Acts 9:15,16). Jesus assured him nothing would happen until he preached in Rome (Acts 23:11).

Were the early Christians wrong in expecting the return of Christ at any time? On the contrary. Because they saw no inconsistency between Jesus' emphasis on the imminence of the Rapture and the necessity of occupying until He comes (Luke 19:13), neither should Christians today.

It seems to please the Lord that the Church in every generation hold a balanced view concerning the time of the Rapture. Its members should look for the Lord's return any day, but keep busy in the meantime.

Christians must avoid being so eager that they set dates for the coming of the Lord. No man knows the day or the hour (Matthew 24:36).

They must also beware of the mistake of the Thessalonians. Some at Thessalonica said that

18

since Christ's return was so near, they need not work anymore. Paul rebuked such an attitude (2 Thessalonians 3:6-11).

However, for Christians to say, "My Lord delays His coming," is equally wrong (Matthew 24:48-51). This attitude promotes sinful conduct and not just idleness. It even leads some to the cynical position of the scoffers, who say: "Where is the promise of his coming? for since the fathers fell asleep, all things continue as they were from the beginning of the creation" (2 Peter 3:4).

As to the reason for Christ's not having already come, Peter says a desire to see sinners saved is behind the delay: "The Lord . . . is long-suffering to us-ward, not willing that any should perish, but that all should come to repentance" (2 Peter 3:9).

Private Versus Public Arrival

Expecting Christ's return momentarily necessitates a distinction between the two phases of His second coming. At the Rapture, His coming will be recognized only by those waiting for Him. As the writer of the Book of Hebrews says: "Unto them that look for him shall he appear" (Hebrews 9:28). But at what theologians call the revelation of Christ, "every eye shall see him" (Revelation 1:7). This includes "all kindreds of the earth."

A summary of the teachings of the Bible on the distinguishing characteristics between the rapture and the revelation of Christ includes the following:

1. At the Rapture Christ will come *for* the saints (1 Thessalonians 4:13-18), while at the Revelation He will come *with* the saints (Jude 14).

2. In the first appearing He will meet His

followers in the air (1 Thessalonians 4:17), but in the second He will descend to earth and stand on Mount Olivet (Zechariah 14:4).

3. The Rapture will occur before the Tribulation, while the Revelation will occur at its end—with at least 7 years between the two.

4. At the Rapture the Lord will come to gather Christians to himself (2 Thessalonians 2:1), while at the Revelation He will come to punish living sinners (2 Thessalonians 1:8).

5. Satan will continue to work after the Rapture (Revelation 12:12), but at the Revelation he will be bound for 1,000 years (Revelation 20:1-3).

Those Left Behind

The Bible makes several plain statements concerning the rapture of the Church. Not long before His departure from earth, Jesus himself said: "I will come again, and receive you unto myself; that where I am, there ye may be also" (John 14:3). He would "receive," transport, or rapture them, taking them where He is. There they would enjoy with Him the wonders of the world to come.

On another occasion, Christ spoke of a split-second separation between saint and sinner at the Rapture (Matthew 24:40,41). Two men will be working together. One will be taken and the other will be left. Two women will be grinding at a mill. One will depart to be with the Lord, but the other will remain to face what follows on earth. Two will be together in bed. One will be taken and the other will be left behind (Luke 17:34).

Some see, in these words, Jesus' warning of the suddenness of judgment in the Tribulation. How-

ever, the triple illustration seems to describe well
the separation of saint from sinner at the Rapture.

On Blinking the Eye

Paul includes some clear statements on the Rapture in his writings. He says the generation of
Christians living at the time of the Rapture will
not need to die. In his words, "We shall not all
sleep" (1 Corinthians 15:51). God will change the
mortal bodies of believers to immortal ones at the
moment Jesus appears.

By definition, a mortal body is subject to death.
Naturally, bodies that are vulnerable to death
cannot rise to meet the Lord in the heavenlies (1
Corinthians 15:53). At the instant of this great
change in the bodies of all living Christians, Paul
says: "Death is swallowed up in victory" (1
Corinthians 15:54).

As he explains the good news of the Rapture to
the Corinthians, the apostle stresses the suddenness of the Rapture. It will be "in a moment" (1
Corinthians 15:52). The Greek word he uses for
moment is the source of the English word *atom*.
Before the development of the atom bomb, the
atom was considered the smallest, and therefore
indivisible, element in the universe. So, Paul is
saying that in the smallest indivisible period of
time the Rapture will occur.

To assist his readers in comprehending this
emphasis, Paul adds that this great change in
believers' bodies will take place "in the twinkling
of an eye." Since most people blink their eyes many
times per minute, the quickness of the event is
made clear.

A Convention in the Sky

Paul provides additional information on the Rapture in his first letter to the Thessalonians (1 Thessalonians 4:13-18). There he shows what happens following the sudden physical change he had written the Corinthians about.

The Thessalonians had been expecting the imminent return of Jesus, and were disturbed that some believers had already died prior to this event. It is obvious that they anticipated being in the generation that would experience the sudden change from mortality to immortality. To answer their questions as to what would happen to those who had died in Christ, the apostle says they will experience resurrection just before the living are raptured.

Then Paul explains that immediately after the resurrection of the dead in Christ, "we which are alive and remain shall be caught up together with them in the clouds, to meet the Lord in the air: and so shall we ever be with the Lord" (1 Thessalonians 4:17). All that is implied in the apostle's reference to living Christians being changed and "caught up" is inherent in the theological definition of the term *Rapture*.

Picturing Future Events

In addition to the specific statements about the Rapture, the Bible also has some pictures of the event in its pages. Picturing, or predicting by example, is a favorite device of Scripture in revealing things to come. For instance, Jesus said: "And as Moses lifted up the serpent in the wilderness, even so must the Son of man be lifted up" (John 3:14).

The translation of Enoch is perhaps the best of the Bible's pictures of the Rapture. The writer of the Book of Hebrews declares: "By faith Enoch was translated that he should not see death; and was not found, because God had translated him" (Hebrews 11:5). For those who hesitate to use the word *rapture* because it is not in Scripture, translation serves as an excellent substitute.

Genesis gives the original account of the ancient prophet's translation. There Moses records: "And Enoch walked with God: and he was not; for God took him" (Genesis 5:24).

Elijah's transportation to heaven in a whirlwind is another picture that serves as a preview of the Rapture (2 Kings 2:11). While still alive, he was changed, caught up, and carried to heaven in a moment. The fact that Elijah landed safely is clear, because he appeared with Jesus on the Mount of Transfiguration centuries later (Mark 9:4).

The New Testament also has a picture of the Rapture—at least of its transportation aspects. Philip the evangelist was caught up and transported by the Spirit from one location to another (Acts 8:39,40). Of course, the future Rapture will be on a much larger scale and will include the change from mortality to immortality, which Philip did not experience. At any rate, the Rapture to come is not without precedent in Scripture.

Preparing for the Trip

The greatest personal benefit from a study of the coming translation concerns being ready to go in the Rapture. Jesus used three parables to provoke proper preparations for the trip.

The Master's famous story of the 10 virgins

focuses on personal preparations for His return (Matthew 25:1-13). In the Parable of the Talents, Jesus exhorts His followers to faithfulness in service while they await His return (Matthew 25:14-30). In the third of the preparation parables, the Lord emphasizes accountability upon His return (Matthew 25:31-46).

Some see the issue of national accountability in the last of these stories. Indeed, in the parable the nations appear before the returning Christ. They are separated into two groups: "sheep" and "goats." The first is rewarded, while the second is punished.

The Bible makes it clear that leaders of nations must account to God for their use or abuse of the power with which the Lord himself entrusted them. Numerous passages of Scripture also show that whole nations must answer to God for their collective conduct.

If national accountability is in view here, Christ's parable suggests one possible basis of judgment: a nation's attitude and behavior toward the Lord's chosen people, Israel. His reference to punishment for mistreatment of "my brethren" could suggest this.

However, before this parable ends, personal accountability is certainly included. As the Judge of those before Him, Jesus says: "Depart from me, ye cursed, into everlasting fire, prepared for the devil and his angels" (Matthew 25:41). While He is addressing a group, the sentence is individual in nature.

To avoid hearing such words, the serious subject of accountability to God for our conduct in this world should stir us all to prepare for the Rapture.

3

A Terrible Time Ahead

Mark 13:19-27

On Being Involved

People in this age seem quick to get involved in causes—causes for better health, better working conditions, civil rights, and numerous others. Most of these involve group action.

However, few people are interested in becoming involved in the lives or problems of other individuals. They are afraid of court appearances, lawsuits, or of a continuing involvement. Some people are witnesses to accidents or acts of violence, but they turn their backs because they fear becoming involved.

For those who do not go with Jesus in the Rapture when He comes for His church, a terrible time is ahead. Through a study of Scripture, one becomes aware of the impending danger. As Paul says, Christians are not of the night that this day should take them unaware (1 Thessalonians 5:3,4). Knowing that "sudden destruction" is just ahead, God's people should become involved and share their insights with their unsaved friends. Unlike those of the world, believers must be involved in efforts to save their fellowmen from the misery of the "tribulation period" foretold in Scripture. This can be done by sharing their faith in Christ with others.

Troublesome Times

There is a sense in which tribulation is the common lot of all Christians. Jesus warned His disciples they would experience trouble in this world (John 16:33). Some would even be killed for His sake (Matthew 24:9). Paul told his converts they "must through much tribulation enter into the kingdom of God" (Acts 14:22). He went so far as to suggest good could come out of suffering for Christ's sake: "Tribulation worketh patience" (Romans 5:3).

But then there is tribulation of a different sort. It comes as punishment on men for their sins. Before the bondage of Israel ended, the Egyptians knew such trouble. Their rivers turned to blood. A plague of frogs moved across the land and filled the houses. Lice covered man and beast. Flies were everywhere. The cattle got sick and died. Painful boils infected men. And "there was hail, ... such as there was none like it in all the land of Egypt since it became a nation .... And the hail smote every herb of the field, and brake every tree of the field" (Exodus 9:24,25). Then, locusts ate what little vegetation was left. Moses writes: "Before them there were no such locusts as they, neither after them shall be such" (Exodus 10:14).

Darkness "which could be felt" covered the land (Exodus 10:21-23). Finally, one fateful night all the firstborn of the land failed to awaken from sleep because of the hand of the death angel.

The Worst Is Yet to Come

Yet, is spite of the intensity of this time of suffering in Egypt (and many other such periods in history), Jesus said there will be another period that will be even worse. Knowing the future as He does, He is too honest with men not to warn them.

The day ahead will bring trouble on top of trouble. As the Master explained to His disciples: "For in those days shall be affliction, such as was not from the beginning of the creation which God created unto this time, neither shall be" (Mark 13:19). Old Testament passages speak of the same event. Jeremiah says: "Alas! for that day is great, so that none is like it" (Jeremiah 30:7). Daniel uses similar words (Daniel 12:1), as does Joel (Joel 2:2).

Sometimes Scripture refers to this period of tribulation as "the day of the LORD"; suggesting a time of great wrath (Joel 2:1,11). In some cases, more immediate judgment is also in view. But the overall teaching of these passages is that history's greatest time of suffering for sin is yet in the future. John refers to it as the "great tribulation" (Revelation 7:14). Literally, he calls it "the tribulation, the great one."

Just as an understanding of a disease assists a person in staying free from it, so knowledge of the Tribulation can help one escape it. There are helpful insights in Scripture concerning the purpose, the length, and the events of the Tribulation.

An Individual Matter

God appears to have specific purposes in allowing this great period of suffering on earth. These purposes are related to individuals, to nations, and, especially, to the Jews.

Individuals left behind at the rapture of the Church will be affected by the events that will follow on the earth. For one thing, people's tendency to sin will, apparently, increase. One of the reasons God has the Church in the world is to restrain evil. With its influence no longer felt after the Rapture, men will think they are freer than ever to live wicked lives.

The depravity of man, his bent toward sinfulness, will be demonstrated at its worst. Evil men will "wax worse and worse" (2 Timothy 3:13). Paul refers to this period as the time of man's great apostasy or falling away (2 Thessalonians 2:3).

Man's conduct will be so bad that God will be altogether just in His swift acts of Tribulation judgment. Focusing on this, Isaiah says:

> Come, my people, enter thou into thy chambers, and shut thy doors about thee: hide thyself as it were for a little moment, until the indignation be overpast. For, behold, the LORD cometh out of his place to punish the inhabitants of the earth for their iniquity (Isaiah 26:20,21).

Still, the Lord does not punish merely for the sake of justice. Because men are yet in time and not eternity, individuals who will may turn to God. In fact, two choice witnesses will try to turn men to God during the Tribulation (Revelation 11:3-12). Then, when adverse circumstances make the preaching of the gospel impossible for men, God will send angels to proclaim it (Revelation 14:6,7,9, 10).

Some will respond favorably to the grace of God

in that hour. Among them will be at least 144,000 Jews (Revelation 7:4) and a great multitude of Gentiles (vv. 9-14). They will form the nucleus for populating the earth during the Millennium. They will survive the Tribulation by God's special protection (12:13-16).

However, a wholesale turning to God during the Tribulation is not indicated. In fact, men in general will be more rebellious against the Lord than ever (Revelation 9:20,21; 16:9,11).

A Family Affair

An even greater purpose of God in the Tribulation concerns the working out of His plan for the family of Israel, the Jews. Central to that plan was the promise of the coming of the Messiah through them. However, when that promise was fulfilled, the people of Israel rejected Him. In persuading the Romans to execute Jesus, the Jewish leaders cried: "His blood be on us, and on our children" (Matthew 27:25). Little did they realize what they were saying.

Punishment was swift. Forty years later the Romans destroyed Jerusalem and burned the temple, and Israel ceased to exist as a nation. Its people were scattered to the four winds. In further judgment on the Jews for their rejection of the Messiah, as well as to bring them to repentance, the Lord has planned the Tribulation. Jeremiah calls this period the "time of Jacob's trouble" (Jeremiah 30:6,7).

The Bible indicates that in the last days the Lord will take up where He left off 2,000 years ago in dealing with the Jews as a people. Through the trials of the Tribulation, He will purify them, so

Jesus, as David's Son, may return to earth and rule over them as King of kings for 1,000 years.

Zechariah foresaw this. Speaking for God, he declared:

> And I will bring the third part through the fire, and will refine them as silver is refined, and will try them as gold is tried: they shall call on my name, and I will hear them: I will say, It is my people: and they shall say, The LORD is my God (Zechariah 13:9).

Of National Concern

However, in the Tribulation the Lord will concern himself with all the nations of the world and not just Israel. At the end of this period, His Son will reign over all the countries of the earth for 1,000 years. Purified Jews will be joined by a remnant of Gentiles from all nations, in worship and service to Jesus.

Speaking of such a future time, an Old Testament prophet proclaims:

> Thus saith the LORD of hosts; In those days it shall come to pass, that ten men shall take hold out of all languages of the nations, even shall take hold of the skirt of him that is a Jew, saying, We will go with you: for we have heard that God is with you (Zechariah 8:23).

The Tribulation will serve the purpose of bringing a remnant of Gentiles to this place of service to God. But prior to this, punishment for national ungodliness will come on the world. A specific sin for which judgment will fall during the Tribulation is an attitude of violent racial prejudice against the Jews. Hitler serves as history's best-known example of those who thought to rid the earth of the sons of Israel. His slaughter of 6 million Jews shows how far a nation can go in anti-Semitism.

Apparently, toward the end of the Tribulation the nations of the earth will follow a new Hitler-like leader's plans for genocide. For this, the nations must answer to God. In referring to this, the Lord says:

> I will also gather all nations, and will bring them down into the valley of Jehoshaphat, and will plead with them there for my people and for my heritage Israel, whom they have scattered among the nations, and parted my land (Joel 3:2).

How Long, Lord?

Scripture indicates the Tribulation will be of relatively short duration. The destruction during its days will be so widespread that if it were a longer period nothing would be left alive on earth. Jesus said: "Except that the Lord had shortened those days, no flesh should be saved: but for the elect's sake, whom he hath chosen, he hath shortened the days" (Mark 13:20).

More specifically, Daniel suggests the Tribulation will last only 7 years. In response to his prayer concerning the end of the 70-year Babylonian captivity, the Lord speaks to the prophet about an important 70-week segment of Israel's future (Daniel 9:24-27). It is obvious these are weeks of years rather than days. The Hebrew word for "weeks" simply means "sevens."

Daniel separates 1 week from the other 69. The 69 weeks run "from the going forth of the commandment to restore and to build Jerusalem, unto the Messiah" (Daniel 9:25). Various Medo-Persian rulers issued different decrees to end the Babylonian captivity of the Jews. However, only one of these specifically legalized the rebuilding of the Holy City. This decree came from Artaxerxes in 445 B.C.

Since the 69 weeks spoken of in Daniel are weeks of *years*, the amount of time involved would total 483 years. However, Bible years consisted of twelve *30-day* months. So, when the 69 weeks are calculated using months of today's length, they total 476 years. Of course, mathematical exactness is impossible because of differences in calendar calculations during the course of history. But 476 years from 445 B.C. takes one to about the time of the crucifixion of Jesus, around A.D. 30.

When Israel showed their rejection of their Messiah by executing Him, the Lord turned to the Gentiles for the time being. This explains the time lapse between the 69th and 70th weeks of Daniel. In the last days, then, God will move to complete His covenant relations with the Jews during Daniel's 70th week.

That the 70th week is of 7 literal years' duration is further indicated by its division in the middle by the Antichrist's great abomination or sin (Daniel 9:27). This act brings the terrible desolation of Tribulation judgment from God in the second part of the 7-year period.

The Bible speaks of this half of the week as "a time, times, and a half" (Daniel 7:25; 12:7), 1260 days (Revelation 12:6), and 42 months (Revelation 11:2; 13:5). With the calendar of twelve 30-day months of the past, each of these clearly describes a 3½-year period.

The First Round

The Bible indicates the first half of the Tribulation will be less severe than the second. Some writers speak of the first part as being a time of the wrath of man and the second as a time of the wrath of God.

Revelation 6 centers on the opening of the seven seals of the book of judgment. Things begin with the arrival of the Antichrist on a white horse. He seems to be a peaceful person with a solution to all earth's problems (vv. 1,2). But suddenly, a red horse appears. Its rider takes peace from the earth (vv. 3,4). Then a famine follows as a black steed arrives on the scene. And with the appearance of a pale horse, one-fourth of the population of the earth dies (vv. 5-8). Worldly men then turn in wrath on those who received God's grace during the early days of the Tribulation. The opening of the fifth seal pictures this persecution (vv. 9-11).

When the sixth seal is opened, men face the wrath of God directly. They pray for the rocks and mountains to fall on them and spare them from their fate (vv. 12-17).

However, before God forces sinful men to drink the wine from the cup of His wrath, the Tribulation saints are sealed for special protection. Revelation 7 describes this. The command of God stays judgment until a company of both Jews and Gentiles receive His guarantee of safety. It seems all this takes place in the middle of the Tribulation.

The Second Round

Chapters 8 through 16 of Revelation show why the beginning of the second round of the Tribulation strikes such terror in the hearts of men. The opening of the seventh seal sanctions the full fury of God's wrath. With the successive blowing of the seven trumpets, the situation on earth grows even worse. But the severest time of all for rebelling men comes as God pours out punishment from seven vials or bottles.

As the Tribulation progresses, the punishments increase in severity. For example, the second trumpet affects one-third of the creatures of the sea, but the second vial affects the entire sea (Revelation 8:8,9; 16:3). The fourth trumpet affects one-third of the sun, moon, and stars, but with the fourth vial the sun becomes intensely hot and burns men as fire (8:12; 16:8,9).

Other Tribulation events include: a large portion of the world's water supply turning to blood, locusts that sting like scorpions tormenting men, and terrible sores that affix themselves to men's bodies. No wonder many seek death, but they cannot find it (Revelation 9:6).

Knowing all this, Jesus urges men to accept His means of escaping the Tribulation: "Watch ye therefore, and pray always, that ye may be accounted worthy to escape all these things that shall come to pass, and to stand before the Son of man" (Luke 21:36).

4

The Man of Deception

REVELATION 13:1-8

A Question of Law and Order

He lived up to his national reputation as one of the best lecturers in the land. The program committee for the city-wide PTA Founders' Day Banquet had made a good selection. What he said was so appealing that everyone listened, even though he spoke for 1½ hours.

The speaker was not a religious person, yet he deplored the moral degeneration in the nation. He obviously had no political ambitions, but he spoke of the breakdown of law and order in the country. While discussing the matter, he told a story that his audience would never forget. It concerned a conversation that had occurred between himself and a taxi driver while traveling from an airport to the site of one of his many speaking engagements.

The two men discussed the nation's needs, particularly those relating to law and order. Suddenly the driver declared, "What we need is an able dictator to take over this country for a while until he, by a strong hand, gets things straightened out!"

The speaker's reply was, "But, sir, did you ever hear of such a person turning things back to the people again after he had restored order in the land?"

Perhaps neither the lecturer nor the driver was aware of what the Bible says about a coming world ruler, yet their conversation provides a clear illustration of how the spirit of the Antichrist is preparing the way for his coming. It is important, therefore, to know what Scripture says about him.

What do the various names given the Antichrist in the Bible reveal about him? What kind of a person will he be? Will he be a successful candidate for the office of King of kings? If elected, to what extent will his programs succeed?

To remain ignorant as to what God has revealed about all this, might predispose one to vote for the wrong person. The Antichrist cannot be the candidate of the Christian's choice.

What's in a Name?

The Antichrist has several names in Scripture. The list of some scholars runs as high as two dozen. These tell something of the kind of person the coming world ruler will be.

One figure used to describe him is that of a "little horn." Daniel uses this term to refer to the Antichrist in both chapters 7 and 8 of his book. The "little horn" of Daniel 8:9 pictures two great personages. The one, Antiochus Epiphanes, came on the scene less than 400 years after Daniel's day. The other, the Antichrist, is yet to come.

In the account, the prophet tells of a "he goat" that appears to him in a vision. The goat has one great horn, which is broken and replaced by four lesser ones. Out of one of these comes the significant title "little horn." After the dream, an angel explains to Daniel that "the rough goat is the king of Grecia: and the great horn that is between his eyes is the first king" (Daniel 8:21). This is an obvious reference to Alexander the Great.

Speaking of what would happen to Alexander's empire after his death, the angel told Daniel the four smaller horns pictured the fact that "four kingdoms [would] stand up out of the nation" (Daniel 8:22). Subsequent history records that one of these was centered in ancient Syria. In time the "little horn" arose to rule over that part of the great Grecian Empire.

A comparison of the details of Daniel's prophecy concerning the activities of the "little horn" (Daniel 8:21-25) with the historical facts of the reign of Antiochus (175-164 B.C.), makes it clear that it is Antiochus of whom Daniel speaks.

Dead or Alive

Located between the Syrian section of ancient Greece, over which Antiochus ruled, and the Egyptian portion of the kingdom, was the little land of Israel. The two fought with each other periodically for control of Palestine. Since the destiny of the Jews was tied up in world affairs, God gave Daniel insight into what was ahead politically.

In keeping with the details of Daniel's prophecy, history records Antiochus' efforts to wipe out the religion of Judaism. When the Jews heard that Antiochus had been killed in a battle with Egypt, they rejoiced and rose up in rebellion against Syria. The report of Antiochus' death, however, turned out to be false. And to put down the uprising and show himself much alive, Antiochus made havoc of the Israelites on his return to Syria through Palestine. He outlawed the possession of Jewish Scripture, the practice of circumcision, and sabbath keeping.

As Daniel had prophesied (Daniel 8:11,12), the king also ordered all sacrifices to Jehovah at the temple to end. In addition, he erected a statue of Zeus, the chief god of the Greeks, in the Holy of Holies, and he commanded the Jews to worship him. Further, in terrible abomination, he sacrificed a swine on the altar of burnt offerings. Thousands of Jews refused to obey the worship command of Antiochus and were slaughtered wholesale.

Little Horn II

But the activities of Antiochus did not exhaust Daniel's prophecy. The fact that the "little horn" would continue until the time of the Messiah makes it clear that another fulfillment is also in view (Daniel 8:25). The Syrian king was a type of the Antichrist to come.

The "little horn" of Daniel 7 speaks exclusively of the future Antichrist. The "little horn" arises from one of the 10 horns of a "fourth beast, dreadful and terrible," of another vision of the prophet (Daniel 7:7,8). History has made it clear that Daniel saw things concerning the great Roman Empire in this revelation.

Daniel's second "little horn" also continues to the time of the Messiah's earthly reign (Daniel 7:20-27). In some way, then, the influences of ancient Rome will remain in world affairs until the end time. Therefore, the person symbolized in the figure is certainly the Antichrist.

Both Antiochus and the Antichrist seem to be in

view again later as Daniel describes a certain "vile person" (Daniel 11:21-45). This is indicated by the fact that he too commits the "abomination of desolation" and also takes away the daily sacrifice.

The Antichrist is further referred to by Daniel as simply "the prince that shall come" (Daniel 9:26). He also causes the sacrifices to cease and commits the abomination of desolation.

Counterfeit Coin

The New Testament uses three significant titles for the coming world ruler. The first of these is the much-used name *Antichrist*. It appears only in the first and second epistles of John, but the apostle uses it five times in these works. The prefix of the word *Antichrist* obviously suggests that the person wearing the title will be "against Christ."

The writer employs the term twice in 1 John 2:18—once in the singular and once in the plural. His readers learn by what he says that in the last days one person will be known as the Antichrist. However, in the course of history, several will come before him who exhibit similar characteristics. Therefore, men will actually witness "many antichrists" along the way.

In 1 John 2:22 the term is applied to followers of his ways more than to the Antichrist himself: "He is antichrist, that denieth the Father and the Son." Accordingly, rejecting the deity of the true Christ is characteristic of the Antichrist. The same is true of a denial of the fact that Christ actually came in the flesh (1 John 4:3; 2 John 7).

But the Greek prefix *anti* conveys the idea of one who "substitutes for" or tries to "stand in the place of" Christ. Jesus warned that many would come claiming to be the Christ (Mark 13:6). However, in the end, one will arise above all others before him and claim to be God (2 Thessalonians 2:4).

To not be deceived, a person should know what the real coin looks like well enough to readily recognize the counterfeit coin. The same is true of Christ and the Antichrist.

On the Most-wanted List

A second title for the Antichrist in the New Testament is the "man of sin" (2 Thessalonians 2:3). Literally, he is "the lawless one." Does this mean he will be the outlaw of outlaws? Will he end up on some "most-wanted" list?

Initially, at least, the Antichrist could gain little following as a notorious lawbreaker. Nor could he get very far as a political leader of men by promoting anarchy. But by the time he reveals his true nature, the coming world ruler will disregard all the laws of God and those of men that are based on righteous principles.

A Beast at Large

John sees the Antichrist as a ferocious beast at large (Revelation 13:1-8) with the features of a leopard, a bear, and a lion. But in spite of what would seem to be a repulsive appearance, the apostle notes: "And all the world wondered after the beast" (Revelation 13:3). Part of the reason for their following him is his miraculous resurrection-like recovery from a "deadly wound."

In another extended passage John says:

And they that dwell on the earth shall wonder,

40

whose names were not written in the book of life from the foundation of the world, when they behold the beast that was, and is not, and yet is (Revelation 17:8).

Dual Personality

Further, men will be attracted to the Antichrist by the appealing side of his "double personality." It seems when he first arrives on the world scene he will be a man of peace. A prophet of old declared that he "by peace shall destroy many" (Daniel 8:25). This corresponds to the entry of the man on the white horse referred to in John's writings (Revelation 6:2).

However, once in power, the coming world ruler will show he is by no means a peace-loving man. Only then will men realize he has tricked them by his "flatteries" (Daniel 11:32).

The Antichrist will apparently possess those smooth personal qualities that will make him a shrewd politician. He will so impress some of the kings of earth with his political genius, that in reckless abandon they will turn their countries over to him (Revelation 17:12,13). Only when it is too late will they realize their mistake. His craftiness will serve his ends well (Daniel 8:25).

Superman

Some Scripture passages suggest the Antichrist will have an impressive physical appearance. Daniel describes him as one "whose look was more stout than his fellows" (Daniel 7:20). The prophet also says he will be a king of fierce or strong countenance (Daniel 8:23).

Further, the Antichrist will appear on the world scene as an intellectual giant. According to Daniel, he will have a capacity for "understanding dark sentences" (Daniel 8:23). Like Solomon of old, the coming world ruler will demonstrate an ability to answer "hard questions" (2 Chronicles 9:1). Perhaps, as with Joseph, his wisdom will be such that men will say of him: "Can we find such a one as this is, a man in whom the Spirit of God is?" (Genesis 41:38). Concluding such, the world will readily turn its affairs over to the Antichrist.

It also seems the Antichrist will possess great powers of persuasion as an orator. The Bible says he will have "a mouth speaking great things" (Daniel 7:8). Scripture also describes him as one with a "mouth as the mouth of a lion" (Revelation 13:2). This may suggest that men will be as impressed with his kingly voice as they are moved when the king of beasts roars in the forest.

History has never been without its demagogues. In his ability to sway men by public speech, Hitler stands as a classic example. But the Antichrist will excel anything world politics has ever produced in an orator. The masses will view him as a real superman.

In his addresses to swelling mobs, the coming world ruler will also speak great blasphemies (Revelation 13:5). Probably he will not do this until later in his reign. Yet, John saw clearly that sometime during his rule over the earth the Antichrist "opened his mouth in blasphemy against God, to blaspheme his name, and his tabernacle, and them that dwell in heaven" (Revelation 13:6).

Wonder of the World

But what an egotistical person the Antichrist

42

will be! Daniel declares: "He shall magnify himself in his heart" (Daniel 8:25). Nothing will feed his ego like being viewed as the wonder of the world. Indeed, he will think of himself as a god and cause others to do the same (Daniel 11:36,37).

In a real sense, the Antichrist will function in a superhuman way. He will yield himself to Satan to such an extent that finally the devil will turn over to him "his power, and his seat, and great authority" (Revelation 13:2). Then, much of what he projects before men will be more than a dynamic human personality. In his person he will be propelled supernaturally. His moment of success will not be due simply to what he is by natural birth and training. Daniel declares: "And his power shall be mighty, but not by his own power: and he shall destroy wonderfully, and shall prosper, and practice" (Daniel 8:24).

Watch Your Focus

Even though the "man of sin" will be such a magnetic and dreadful person, none need fear him. All may choose Christ over the Antichrist and not be left behind when the Lord comes for His own.

Every sinner should be like the young employee who was learning to operate a locomotive. His trainer, a Christian engineer, said, "I want to teach you how to run this thing as quickly as I can. You see, I'm expecting Jesus to come, and I may be raptured out of my seat any moment." The young man's immediate reply was, "Man, don't tell me how to operate the engine of a train. Just explain to me how to go with you when Christ returns."

To focus on the Antichrist and be unduly frightened is also to forget that the Bible predicts an awful and speedy end for him. He is even called the "son of perdition" (2 Thessalonians 2:3). Perdition speaks of "utter ruin, destruction, or irretrievable loss." This does not imply that he is so predestined to ruin that he has no choice. Rather, two Scripture verses say he will *deliberately* "go into perdition" (Revelation 17:8,11).

In the end, the Antichrist will be helpless before the Almighty. Daniel declares: "He shall be broken without hand" (Daniel 8:25). Almost in pity Daniel says further: "He shall come to his end, and none shall help him" (11:45).

Daniel also sees the lawless one "slain, and his body destroyed, and given to the burning flame" (7:11). This follows on the direct orders of the Ancient of Days, the Messiah, and is specifically done because of the blasphemous words the beast speaks against God.

Paul says the Lord will destroy the "man of sin" by the brightness of His coming (2 Thessalonians 2:8). Thus, He will cut short the terrible things the Antichrist is doing on earth. God is always in control, even when He allows suffering to come to men for a season.

In a vision, John learns the final fate of the Antichrist. He is cast alive into the lake of fire (Revelation 19:20), where he is "tormented day and night for ever and ever" (20:10).

What is the value of a study about the person and evil works of the Antichrist? It makes one aware of the subtle influences of the spirit of lawlessness at work in the world today. By being informed, one can cast his vote for a different candidate. He can choose Christ over the Antichrist and be saved.

5

A Reign of Terror

REVELATION 13:11-18

The People's Choice

As the hour approached for the big event, hundreds of people filled the courthouse square in the county seat town. A group of hill folk played and sang bluegrass music. The crowd munched on free hot dogs and sipped cold lemonade. Laughter as well as lively talk of farming, business, and politics filled the air.

The central committee of one of the county's political parties was sponsoring the affair. Candidates for offices small and large circulated among the people in the customary handshaking ritual. In between numbers from the bluegrass band, they asked for votes and made speeches about what they would do if elected. Each spoke in his turn, beginning with the candidates for the least important offices, up to those running for the most important ones.

Finally, the big moment arrived. Amid cheers from the crowd, the candidate for governor mounted the small platform under a giant oak on the courthouse lawn. Silence settled over the audience as he reached the podium.

With evangelistic fervor, the political aspirant made his promises. If elected, he would see that the unemployment rate dropped. He would conquer the monster inflation. Schoolteachers would get a long overdue raise. He guaranteed there would be an increase in old-age pensions and twice as much free health care as before. Income for farmers would rise dramatically.

When the speech ended, men shouted and threw their hats into the air. Here was a man they could wholeheartedly vote for. He owed no special interest groups. He was the people's choice.

The Dawn of a New Day

In efforts to gain the favor of the voters, present-day politicians differ little from those of yesterday. Historians say Caesar Augustus stood on a political platform much like that of the candidate in the modern welfare state. He promised that during his reign none would go hungry. There would be plenty of consumer goods, and all would have the money to buy them. This would be accomplished through vast public works programs. He would deal successfully with the health problems of the empire. Law and order would prevail in the land. Little wonder, then, that his subjects offered him divine worship.

Not unlike past and present politicians, the future candidate for the office of world ruler will present a most appealing platform. The programs of the Antichrist will encompass all the major areas of life for the people of planet earth. His efforts to solve the world's problems will center on economics, religion, and politics. In each of these he will offer the dawn of a new day.

World Peace

One of the planks in the political platform of the Antichrist will concern the age-old problem of war. What is it that men fight over more than anything else in the world? Why, it is land, of course. Neighbors in cities go to court in disputes over a few feet of boundary lines between lots. Farmers battle over the exact location of ancient landmarks. Nations go to war over questions concerning control of territory.

So, the Antichrist will reason, what is the best way to rid the earth of the ancient scourge of war? It is obvious. Get rid of all national boundary lines. Unite the world politically under one government. Patriotism to its one flag will bind men together. The Bible indicates that countries will voluntarily surrender their national sovereignty in favor of such a plan to outlaw war on the globe (Revelation 17:12,13).

Some educators now call for curricular courses in history departments that show how to make the United Nations into a real world government. While that agency may or may not prove to be the seat of government for the coming world ruler, obviously the spirit of the Antichrist is presently setting the stage for his appearance.

Doing as the Romans

The rule of the Antichrist is related to that of ancient Rome, the last of the great world empires. This was revealed to Daniel as he interpreted Nebuchadnezzar's dream many centuries ago (Daniel 2:40-45).

In the dream, the king saw a colossal figure of a

man made of various metals. Its legs of iron represented the then-to-come world government of Rome. Its two legs foretold the splitting of the great empire into the Eastern and Western divisions, as history has long since recorded. It is significant that the world, even in modern times, remains divided ideologically into these two very camps.

The feet and toes of the great image hold meaning for the end time, including the days of the Antichrist. With his supernatural leadership abilities, he will bring about the union of a divided world. Yet it will be only a surface unity, as signified by the efforts to mix iron and clay in the feet of the image (Daniel 2:41-43). A weak structure is inevitable when men sacrifice principle for the sake of organizational oneness.

The 10 toes on the feet of the image represent at least 10 nations over which the Antichrist will rule. This fact is further suggested by the 10 horns of the beast in Daniel 7:7, as well as those of Revelation 13:1 and 17:12,13.

Since the Antichrist arises as the "little horn" out of these, many see evidence to suggest a revival of ancient Rome in the end time, with its original 10 confederated kingdoms. However, the toes on the feet of the image in Daniel may simply suggest that nations from both the Eastern and Western camps of the world will be loosely united in the last days. Perhaps all that is implied in the prophecy is that the spirit of ancient Rome will remain a force in world politics up to the time of the Antichrist.

Whatever the case, it is clear the domain of the man of sin will eventually be worldwide. Not only will all the world wonder after the beast (Revelation 13:3), but also, John says: "Power [will be] given him over all kindreds, and tongues, and nations" (13:7). The Antichrist will lead the armies of all the nations on earth against heaven's armies at Armageddon (16:14; 19:19).

War on Poverty

It seems the Antichrist will further reason that a second thing over which men fight is money. He may suggest that an unequal distribution of the world's wealth is at the heart of many of earth's difficulties, and that hungry men can be expected to attack. Another way, then, to solve the world's problems is to call for sweeping economic changes.

As a type of the Antichrist, Antiochus Epiphanes followed similar economic policies in almost reckless abandon. For example, Daniel prophesied that he would "scatter among them the prey, and spoil, and riches" (Daniel 11:24). History records that Antiochus often distributed the spoils of battle among the people of Syria. At times he would rush into the streets, throw handfuls of coins into a crowd, and say, "Let him take it to whom fortune sends it."

Happiness Now

According to Greek philosophy, one of man's chief goals in life is to develop and satisfy the physical. Antiochus personified that ideal. He believed men should seek material success and sensual pleasure. "Happiness now!" was his cry.

The promotion of pleasure under Antiochus brought a rash of activity to boost the economy. He built great gymnasiums where the people could come and have fun. The Greeks played many of their games in the nude. In the Greek, gymnasium means "nude." Such things remind one of the last days when men will be "lovers of pleasures more than lovers of God" (2 Timothy 3:4).

Perhaps picturing further what the Antichrist will do in the field of economics, Antiochus made his capital, Antioch of Syria, a beautiful and brilliant city. He erected Greek cities in Palestine as well. The story of the building boom of his day reads like that of many parts of the modern world.

World Economy

It seems the Antichrist will also attract a following by drawing attention to the problem of the world's differing monetary systems. No doubt he will argue, "If one world politically is necessary for peace, then one world economically is necessary for prosperity." With such a common sense philosophy he will develop some kind of world economic and monetary system.

Revelation 18 seems to picture the world economy under the Antichrist. The merchants of the earth get rich in trade with "Babylon." The chapter suggests the economy of the last days will reach a pinnacle of success. Under the Antichrist men may say, "We have finally conquered the age-old financial woes of the world. Ours is a strong, healthy economy. No more stock market crashes. No more economic depressions. No more inflation. Utopia at last!"

Mark of the Beast

But the apparent success of the world economic system under the Antichrist will not be without its price. It appears the man of sin will successfully argue that his economic system must have controls. To enjoy its benefits the balance between supply and demand will need regulation. Prices will have to be stabilized.

With different standards of living on the various parts of the earth, the monetary value of goods sometimes differs radically. This is a real cause of friction between nations. No doubt the world ruler will declare that this cannot continue. Trade must flow freely between countries. The monetary value of goods should be determined on the world market.

Although men may rejoice for a moment in the apparent economic success of the new world of the Antichrist, Scripture reveals it will lead to a terrible day for earth's inhabitants. The economic Babylon of Revelation 18 will fall. Earth's merchants will weep. And finally, the controls of the new system will lead to the mark of the beast. John says the day will come when all men, small or great, rich or poor, bond or free, must receive such a mark in their right hand or on their foreheads. "And ... no man might buy or sell, save he that had the mark, or the name of the beast, or the number of his name" (Revelation 13:17).

Holy Wars

A third area of frequent problems on earth is that of religion. No doubt the Antichrist will capitalize on the fact that all too often men have fought over devoutly held beliefs in so-called "holy wars." From such a base, it seems he will call for drastic changes in the world's religions.

However, knowing that many people are indeed disposed to die for their faith, it seems the Antichrist will not start his reign with this plank in his platform. Rather, in the beginning he will gain favor by practicing religious tolerance. He will guarantee religious freedom in his administration. Daniel states that he will specifically make a covenant with the Jews to that end (Daniel 9:27).

But soon the true religious colors of the Antichrist will appear. He will show where he really stands on religious freedom by breaking the covenant with the Jews just 3½ years after signing it (Daniel 9:27). Then his "holy war" will begin.

Religious Unity

Concluding that religion can serve as a unifying rather than a divisive force if handled correctly, the Antichrist apparently will set out to make it a tool of state. Reasoning that to unify religion must be one, he will determine to combine the world's major faiths into one state church. The Babylon of Revelation 17 seems to picture the result of his efforts.

The Antichrist will unite under his power all religious groups that have drifted away from the truth of God's Word. It seems even those who have held the fundamentals of the faith but perhaps have drifted from them will be included in the church of the Antichrist. Because they believe in the Bible's miracles, they will be deceived by the religious power of the beast.

Jesus warned that in the last days false prophets will arise and "show great signs and wonders" (Matthew 24:24). Paul revealed that the Antichrist's coming will be "after the working of Satan with all power and signs and lying wonders" (2 Thessalonians 2:9).

Present calls for global religious unity suggest that even the non-Christian religions will join the world church of the last days. Muslims, apostate Jews, Hindus, other Eastern religions, and Satan worshipers will join as one.

The great world church will be headed by the false prophet, the religious assistant to the Antichrist. To influence men to join, he will perform noted wonders, call fire down from heaven, and cause an image of the beast to miraculously talk (Revelation 13:13-15).

Religious Persecution

However, not all will cooperate with the world church. Therefore, the Antichrist's earlier religious tolerance will turn to persecution. He "shall wear out the saints of the Most High" (Daniel 7:25). He will destroy the "mighty and the holy people" (Daniel 8:24). He will make war on those loyal to God and overcome them (Revelation 13:7). The false prophet will cause all who refuse to join the world church to be killed (Revelation 13:15).

Before he is through, the Antichrist will renounce all religions and all gods (Daniel 11:36-39). He will speak great blasphemies against the one true God (Revelation 13:5,6). He will even declare himself to be God, and sit in the temple and demand worship as such (2 Thessalonians 2:4). In the end, he will have the audacity to stand against the true Christ, the Prince of princes (Daniel 8:25).

Hindering Force

But when Paul writes the Thessalonians about the Antichrist, his real message is that God is in control—both before the lawless one arrives, and even after he appears. Paraphrasing the apostle's words: Only he who now hinders will continue to restrain until he is taken out of the way. And then shall that wicked one be revealed (2 Thessalonians 2:6-8). Then, and only when on schedule in the outworking of God's plan for the ages, will the Antichrist be allowed to appear.

Just the mere mention of the Antichrist's coming, even in the permissive will of God, causes Paul to quickly note that the Antichrist will soon be destroyed (2 Thessalonians 2:8). Paul's message is meant to comfort, not to frighten.

A Word to the Wise

Following Paul's example, the Church must not dwell on the subject of the Antichrist and his evil works. The message is Christ, not the Antichrist. But prayerful consideration of what the Bible says about the man of sin will keep the Christian on course in the last days. He must not get caught up in the spirit of the age which prepares the way for the beast.

Who is happy with Christianity's many divisions? Would anyone not like to see an end to poverty? Does anyone want war? The Christian wants all the Antichrist will offer, but he refuses to go along with those who say men can have these things by their own efforts and apart from God. Prevailing sin in the hearts of men prevents it.

What all men want, only Christ can permanently give. Paul warns: "For when they shall say, Peace and safety; then sudden destruction cometh upon them, as travail upon a woman with child; and they shall not escape" (1 Thessalonians 5:3).

6

Choosing the Right Side

1 THESSALONIANS 5:1-11

Famous Ruins

Excitement ran high as the group of American tourists neared the ruins of ancient Corinth. Their bus had barely rolled to a stop before eager feet descended its steps to the ground and walked down a short stairway leading to the uncovered ruins of the Biblical site.

On a hill at the left was a sleepy little village housing only a few dozen people. It gave little hint of the population of over half a million souls who had lived there in New Testament times. Ancient Corinth had been a busy commercial center when Paul evangelized there in the first century.

On the right, the tourists saw the remaining upright columns of the temple of Apollo. Men had sacrificed animals to that god there in the days of Paul's ministry. In front of the group, on a high hill overlooking the ruins of Corinth, were fragments of the temple of Aphrodite, the Greek goddess of love. In ancient times, the temple had housed a thousand so-called "sacred" prostitutes. Worshipers had sought union with the goddess through immoral relations with them.

Open Court

Among the ruins of the shops, meat markets, and Roman baths was a famous set of steps. The short stairway had originally led to a building housing offices for the governor of the province. In fact, it is believed these were the very steps Paul was dragged to when he appeared before the governor, who sat as judge on a small platform at the top of the stairs. (Luke records the story in Acts 18.)

The Romans not only believed justice must be done, but also that it should be done openly for the benefit of all. Thus, they often conducted an open court.

The New Testament also speaks of judgment. Paul says all Christians must appear before God one day to account to the Master for the quality of their Christian service on earth (2 Corinthians 5:10). Most likely this will occur in heaven, sometime during the 7 years between the rapture of the Church and the revelation of Jesus. The necessity of having time for such an opportunity is one reason for believing the Church will escape the Tribulation. In addition, there are both scriptural illustrations and promises that God will keep His own out of that period of trouble.

Among the various views, the theological position that the Church will be spared from the Great Tribulation appears the most Biblical. Scholars have compiled impressive lists of evidence in support of the teaching. For example, one writer gives 50 reasons why he believes the Church will not go through the Tribulation.

Escaping God's Way

Basic to the belief that the Church will escape

the Tribulation are scriptural promises such as those found in the Gospels, the Epistles, and the Book of Revelation.

The third Gospel contains the very words of Jesus regarding escaping the terrible time ahead God's way (Luke 21:34-46). His provision for protection from the judgment to come includes watchfulness, correct conduct, and prayer on the part of the believer, and, above all, the grace of God. According to Jesus, if a person wants to avoid the Tribulation he should watch and take heed to himself. He must guard his own heart that it be not "overcharged" with such gross sins as drunkenness (Luke 21:34). He also needs to beware that evils such as "surfeiting," carousing, reveling, or participating in wild parties where alcoholic drinking occurs, do not dull his senses. New Testament Christians avoided such orgies (1 Peter 4:3,4).

But the Lord also warned against letting the legitimate "cares of this life" crowd out the spiritual in one's mind. Being so concerned about the temporal that a person has no time for thoughts of the eternal is a real danger against which all should guard. Jesus said a lack of seriousness about the things that really matter in this world could allow the Tribulation period to "come upon [one] unawares" (Luke 21:34,35). Certainly, the unbelievers of earth will be caught in it as an animal is unsuspectingly snared in a trap.

The Master also encouraged specific prayer that one might "escape all these things that shall come to pass" (Luke 21:36). The implication is, of course, that God will be pleased to grant such a petition.

In mentioning that a person should seek to "be accounted worthy to escape" the Tribulation, Jesus is not teaching that one can gain the Rapture by works. Some have overemphasized such preparation exhortations and declared a partial-Rapture theory. They teach that only the most spiritual will go with Jesus when He comes.

But all living Christians will rise to meet Him. Only by God's grace will each believer be "worthy" to go in the Rapture and "to stand [acceptably] before the Son of man" (Luke 21:36).

Hoping for the Best

The Epistles also contain promises that the Christians alive at the Rapture will thereby escape the Tribulation. Paul refers to the return of Christ as a "blessed hope" (Titus 2:13). Of course, Biblical hope is not the same as the wishful thinking of ordinary men. By definition, the Greek word used in the Bible for hope speaks more of absolute certainty.

Logic argues that the return of the Lord could hardly be viewed as a "blessed" hope if the awfulness of the Tribulation preceded it. How could one look forward to it if he knew he must first face the worst time of trouble ever on earth? Moreover, it is illogical to think that God would pour out His wrath on His church. The Epistles declare that He will not.

In his first letter to the Thessalonians, Paul tells the recently founded church that none in its ranks should think of any kind of coming wrath as they wait for God's Son from heaven (1 Thessalonians 1:10). Jesus delivers believers from the fear of wrath to come. Before concluding his letter to the church, Paul returns again to the subject of the Great Tribulation. In referring to the world, he

58

declares that sudden destruction shall come upon *them* and *they* shall not escape (1 Thessalonians 5:3,4). The contrast of the Christian's position with that of the unbeliever implies that the Christian will escape.

Paul continues the discussion and, as in other similar passages, exhorts his readers to prepare themselves for the Rapture. He ends with the promise: "For God hath not appointed us to wrath, but to obtain salvation by our Lord Jesus Christ" (1 Thessalonians 5:9). With words like these, the Christian hopes for, and is certain of, the best, not the worst. He looks for the coming of Christ, not the Antichrist.

God's Keeping Power

The Book of Revelation also contains a promise that the Church will not have to go through the Tribulation. This promise came originally to the first-century church at Philadelphia in Asia Minor:

> Because thou hast kept the word of my patience, I also will keep thee from the hour of temptation, which shall come upon all the world, to try them that dwell upon the earth (Revelation 3:10).

In addition to whatever meaning the verse may have had for the future of the believers at Philadelphia, it seems intended for universal application. In this passage, Jesus says the trial ahead "shall come upon *all the world*." It would not be localized in Philadelphia. Furthermore, it would be no ordinary period of tribulation. Its severity and scope would test all on earth.

From such testing the Lord promises to keep His own. He will spare them from experiencing the very hour, period, or time of tribulation. Certainly, He does not speak of bringing them safely *through* it; although, naturally, He is capable of doing that instead, if that were His plan.

Thousand-word Pictures

The fact is, God appears to have made special plans for two groups of people during the Tribulation. The one group He will *keep out of* the Tribulation, and the other group He will protect from the awful sufferings of those days and bring safely *through* the Tribulation. These truths become evident when we study some of the pictures given in the Bible.

The Lord's plan for keeping the Church from the very period of tribulation is illustrated in what happened at Sodom and Gomorrah. Abraham prayed for mercy for his spiritually indifferent nephew Lot. God responded favorably. Accordingly, the angel of destruction told Lot he could do nothing until the patriarch's nephew was safely out of the area (Genesis 19:22).

If the storm of divine wrath could not descend on Sodom until "compromising" Lot was out, how much more will this be true of faithful Christians living near the time of the Tribulation?

But God's plan for preserving those who turn to Him during the fires of the Tribulation is also illustrated in Scripture. The Book of Exodus contains miraculous details of how the Lord allowed none of the plagues of Egypt to touch His people in the area of the country where they lived. For example, in recounting the plague of hail, Moses says: "Only in the land of Goshen, where the children of Israel were, was there no hail" (Exodus 9:26).

The Flood serves as another illustration of the different provisions for the two groups. Enoch pictures the Church being raptured before tragedy strikes. Noah and his family provide an example of those preserved by God through a time of unprecedented trouble on earth.

Lessons From the Past

It seems reasonable, then, to conclude that Christians living near the time of the Great Tribulation will be spared its sorrows by being "translated" from earth as Enoch was. God's plan for rapturing the believers appears in Paul's first letter to the Thessalonians. Both the fact that Christians will be translated and the fact that this will occur before the Tribulation were a source of great comfort to the Thessalonians (1 Thessalonians 4:17,18; 5:9-11).

However, apparently another group will come into a relationship with the Lord after the Rapture and will be preserved through the Tribulation. Both Jews and Gentiles will be included in this group.

At a point where the terribleness of the Tribulation is about to begin, John sees four angels who have power to hurt the earth and sea (Revelation 7:1,2). A fifth angel appears who has custody of the great seal of Almighty God. Addressing the angels of destruction, he says: "Hurt not the earth, neither the sea, nor the trees, till we have sealed the servants of our God in their foreheads" (7:3). There then follows the sealing of 144,000 Jews, 12,000 from each tribe.

The protection provided by this sealing may be what is described later by John in Revelation 12.

Perhaps a Jewish remnant is symbolized by the sun-clothed woman that John writes about. A red dragon was about to destroy her, but "the woman fled into the wilderness, where she hath a place prepared of God, that they should feed her there a thousand two hundred and threescore days" (Revelation 12:6).

John continues his description of the dragon's efforts to persecute the woman: "And the [dragon] cast out of his mouth water as a flood after the woman, that he might cause her to be carried away of the flood" (v. 15). But the earth opened and swallowed up the water. Again the apostle says that she escaped to the wilderness and was miraculously nourished "for a time, and times, and half a time" (v. 14).

Getting a New Start

With obvious references to the last 3½ years of the Tribulation, perhaps this passage gives a hint as to how God will feed the remnant of Jews that turn to Him during those dark days. Otherwise, to buy food, they would have to take the mark of the beast and seal their doom.

Gentiles are also included among those miraculously preserved from destruction. John saw "a great multitude, which no man could number, of all nations, and kindreds, and people, and tongues, ... which came out of great tribulation" (Revelation 7:9,14).

To start anew after the Flood, the Lord preserved four couples of the family of man, along with sets of male and female animals, in Noah's ark. It seems that during the Tribulation He will also mercifully protect a remnant of Jews and Gentiles who believe on Jesus after the rapture of the Church. This remnant will be preserved for the new beginning in the Millennium. There must be people on earth to populate it anew.

Coming to a Conclusion

It is true, of course, that various scholars reach differing conclusions as to the time of the Rapture. Among the views, three are most frequently mentioned. Some say the Rapture will occur before the Tribulation begins. Others hold that it will happen in the middle of the 7-year period. Still others contend that it will come at the end of the time of great trouble.

Of the three views, the first seems to be the most scriptural and logical. Theologians have propagated the pre-Tribulation view of the Rapture since earliest times. Irenaeus, an Early Church father, taught that the Tribulation would not begin until the Church is caught away. Hermas, apparently a writer of the same period, declared that the righteous would escape the Tribulation. Other Early Church writings speak of the possibility of Jesus' return at any time, with no thought of the Tribulation coming first.

More current creeds of some church bodies consider anything but the pre-Tribulation position as encouraging complacency among Christians. If Christ cannot come before the Antichrist, why worry about being ready now? His return is at least 3½ to 7 years away. Such views promote the date-setting tendencies the Lord warned about (Mark 13:32,33).

7

He's Coming Again!

ACTS 1:9-11

The Best of Both Worlds

Their bodies were wrinkled and stooped with age, but never was there a more beautiful couple. As Christians, they had grown old gracefully. For over 50 years she had been a lay preacher of the gospel, and he had stood faithfully at her side.

They owned a small duplex and lived in one of the apartments. Through word and deed they were such effective witnesses that none who occupied the other apartment had ever moved out without becoming born-again, Spirit-filled Christians, regardless of what their religious background had been when they moved in.

A young evangelist was holding meetings in their church, and the aged disciples invited him to their apartment for food and fellowship. The group talked of the return of Jesus to earth. The youthful preacher expressed an opinion that the most blessed of hopes was that of going in the Rapture. That way one would never have to know the darkness of walking through the valley of the shadow of death.

The older couple listened patiently to the evangelist's remarks. When he finished, the Christian lady said, "Yes, but, my brother, there is just something about the thought of coming forth from the grave that thrills me through and through!" For her, the resurrection was the greatest hope.

Paul recognized the importance of both the Rapture and the resurrection. He declared that God has it planned so that "whether we wake or sleep, we should live together with him" (1 Thessalonians 5:10). Then, whether the Christian is alive or dead at the return of Christ, he will have the best of both worlds.

The Rapture will occur before the Tribulation. Both living and dead saints will rise to meet the Lord in the air. Then, some 7 years later, at what theologians call the revelation of Christ, they will return with Him to earth to bring to an end the miseries of mankind.

A Royal Welcome

On one occasion as Jesus entered Jerusalem, some gave Him a royal welcome (Mark 11:7-10). They made a carpet of palm branches for His pathway. But a few days later they crucified Him.

Soon Christ will return to earth with a different purpose. This time He will come to reign as King of kings for 1,000 years. His will be a real red-carpet arrival next time.

The Bible gives promises of the second coming of Christ, contains prayers for His soon return, and describes both the joy and sorrow saints and sinners will experience. Sad to say, His revelation to men of earth does not hold the same hopes for all. Prepared ones anticipate it with joy. Those who are not ready tremble with fear at the thought.

Crying Over the Past

Among the Biblical promises, Zechariah speaks of both the first and second comings of Jesus. Of the first, he says: "O daughter of Jerusalem: behold, thy King cometh unto thee: he is just, and having salvation; lowly, and riding upon an ass, and upon a colt the foal of an ass" (Zechariah 9:9). According to Matthew, Jesus fulfilled this prophecy (Matthew 21:4,5). Israel received its King for a moment, but then crucified Him.

Concerning the Second Coming, Zechariah declares that when the Jews see Jesus again they will weep over their past deeds in rejecting their Messiah. He writes: "They shall look upon me whom they have pierced, and they shall mourn for him, as one mourneth for his only son" (Zechariah 12:10).

However, their weeping will be more than just one of regret for past mistakes. It will occur as a result of the grace of God being poured out upon them. Remnants of other nations will join the Jews in a time of worldwide repentance. Matthew says: "And then shall all the tribes of the earth mourn, and they shall see the Son of man coming in the clouds of heaven with power and great glory" (Matthew 24:30).

John ties these Old and New Testament passages together. He writes: "Behold, he cometh with clouds; and every eye shall see him, and they also which pierced him: and all kindreds of the earth shall wail because of him" (Revelation 1:7).

Since these events cannot possibly be associated with anything that happened during Jesus' life on earth, they obviously refer to His second coming. Moreover, they clearly speak of a time when He will be revealed to all mankind. Therefore, they cannot relate to His secret coming for His saints, at which time they will rise to meet Him in the air. These are promises of the Revelation and not the Rapture.

Punishment or Pardon?

Another Old Testament prophet also speaks of the two comings of Jesus—and virtually in the same breath. Without separating the two in his mind, Isaiah says He will come "to proclaim the acceptable year of our LORD," as well as "the day of vengeance of our God" (Isaiah 61:1,2). He will both pardon and punish.

In a combined account, Isaiah predicts the entire earthly ministry of Jesus. God does not permit him to see that the pardoning and punishing aspects of His Son's ministry will occur in two different comings to earth, which will be separated by a long time span.

Isaiah is like a man who stands on one mountain peak and looks across and sees other peaks that appear rather close together, but cannot see the wide valleys hidden from his view that separate them by miles. Like other prophets, he did not fully understand all he wrote under the inspiration of the Spirit (1 Peter 1:10-12).

However, in a synagogue service in Nazareth, Jesus indicated that He had come the first time only to engage in a pardoning ministry. When He read from the Book of Isaiah, He stopped short of including the reference to the "day of vengeance" (Luke 4:16-19). By closing the book where He did, He could truthfully say, "This day is this Scripture fulfilled in your ears" (Luke 4:21).

Jesus will declare the day of vengeance when He comes to earth a second time. Paul indicates that it is precisely for this reason that He will return. Jesus will come "in flaming fire taking vengeance on them that know not God, and that obey not the gospel" (2 Thessalonians 1:8).

Truth Beyond Question

Jesus spoke in parables of His return to this world to establish an earthly kingdom. He began one such story by saying: "A certain nobleman went into a far country to receive for himself a kingdom, and to return" (Luke 19:12). Before the man departed, he gave various amounts of money to several servants for their management while he was away. Upon his return, he called each to give an account. The success or failure of each man's investment practices determined his role in the future administration of the nobleman's estate.

But perhaps the most easily understood promise of Christ's return came at the moment the resurrected Son of God ascended to heaven. Bewildered disciples stood looking intently as Jesus disappeared in a cloud. Suddenly, two angels appeared among them. With the clearest of words they said: "This same Jesus, which is taken up from you into heaven, shall so come in like manner as ye have seen him go into heaven" (Acts 1:11).

Their message of hope declared the truth of the second coming of the Lord beyond question. His coming is certain. As the angels said, "This same Jesus shall come." He will return personally. It will be "this same Jesus," the angels assured the wondering disciples. His return will be a visible event. To the stunned followers of the Lord, the angels declared that He will return "in like manner as ye have seen him go into heaven."

Confusing the Issue

With such a clear promise of Christ's literal return to earth, it is interesting how some try to explain it away. A few writers declare that the promise was fulfilled with the coming of the Lord in the person of the Holy Spirit at Pentecost (Acts 2:1-4). But the Spirit is "another Comforter" (John 14:16,17), and not "this same Jesus." Moreover, Epistles written long after the great event on the Day of Pentecost speak of Christ's coming as yet future (Titus 2:13; 1 Peter 1:7,13; 2 Peter 3:10).

Since judgment is associated with the second coming of Christ, some say the promise of His return was fulfilled by the destruction of Jerusalem in A.D. 70. But in coming to earth a second time, the Lord will execute judgment on sinners worldwide; punishment will not be localized in Jerusalem. John wrote his last book about 25 years after the capital of Israel fell to the Romans. He declared that the Second Coming judgment was yet future (Revelation 6:12-17).

Still others try to apply promises of the second coming of Christ to what happens to the sinner at conversion. Jesus did say He would come to anyone who would open his heart's door (Revelation 3:20). But, as glorious as that experience is, it can hardly qualify as the time when the Lord returns to earth to be with all His children. Efforts like these to spiritualize literal promises of Scripture simply confuse the issue of the Second Coming.

Some even go so far as to say that predictions of

Christ's coming are related to the end of the believer's life in this world. To them the Second Coming is the Lord coming to walk with the Christian through the valley of the shadow of death, as the Psalmist anticipated (Psalm 23:4).

However, Paul declares that Christ's coming will be after the death of many of His followers. They will arise from the dead at the moment of His return (1 Thessalonians 4:13-17). Those who are still alive will actually escape the experience of death at the Second Coming.

Keeping Promises

Reading the promises of a literal, visible, bodily return of Jesus to earth causes many to pray that the day will soon come. For example, John gives the promise: "Behold, he cometh with clouds: and every eye shall see him" (Revelation 1:7). John's response to his own message is immediate and like that of many in modern times. He simply says, "Even so, Amen."

Toward the end of his last book, John again gives assurances of Christ's return to earth. He writes: "He which testifieth these things saith, Surely I come quickly" (Revelation 22:20). Once more the apostle responds to the promise with a prayer: "Amen. Even so, come, Lord Jesus."

Even those in paradise who await the resurrection are anxious about the Second Coming. They join with those who are praying on earth about the matter. John saw the souls of martyrs at rest under heaven's altar and heard them say: "How long, O Lord, holy and true, dost thou not judge and avenge our blood on them that dwell on the earth?" (Revelation 6:10).

Tomorrow's Joy

The second coming of Christ at His revelation holds bright prospects for many. John paints a thrilling picture of Jesus riding on a white horse and leading the armies of heaven: "And the armies which were in heaven followed him upon white horses, clothed in fine linen, white and clean" (Revelation 19:14). The believer's joy becomes almost unspeakable at the thought that he will be included in that great host!

Several different Greek words are necessary for New Testament writers to describe the glories of Christ's return. One common word used to speak of the event is *erchomai*. This Greek verb means simply, "I come." Jesus himself used this word when He said, "I will come again" (John 14:3). Concerning the prophetic element in the Communion service, Paul declares: "Ye do show the Lord's death till he come" (1 Corinthians 11:26).

A second Greek verb employed to describe the return of Christ is *phaneroo*, "I appear." Paul says: "When Christ, who is our life, shall appear, then shall ye also appear with him in glory" (Colossians 3:4).

A noun used by New Testament writers to depict the return of the Lord is *parousia*. It describes the coming, the arrival, or simply the presence of a person. Seventeen of the twenty-four times it appears in Scripture it speaks of the second coming of Christ.

Paul prayed that the Thessalonians would "be preserved blameless unto the coming [literally, 'presence'] of our Lord Jesus Christ" (1 Thessalonians 5:23). Peter exhorts Christians to look for and hasten toward the coming or presence of the

Lord (2 Peter 3:12). John encourages believers to so live that they will not be ashamed in the presence of Jesus upon His return (1 John 2:28).

Another Greek noun depicting the Second Coming is *apokalupsis*. The word refers to an uncovering or disclosure of something and is generally translated by the English word *revelation*.

Paul speaks of the day "when the Lord Jesus shall be revealed from heaven with his mighty angels" (2 Thessalonians 1:7). Peter tells believers to be sober-minded in anticipation of the grace they will receive "at the revelation of Jesus Christ" (1 Peter 1:13). He also talks of the joy of the Christian "when his [Christ's] glory shall be revealed" (1 Peter 4:13).

Nothing to Look Forward To

But while John indicates the joy of victory for the saints at the revelation of Jesus, he also shows it will be a day of great defeat for sinners (Revelation 19:17-21). For them the prospects of the Second Coming are nothing to look forward to. The picture the apostle paints of the glorious return of the Lord to declare war on the men of the earth appears dismal to those whom He will attack.

Christ and His army of saints will do battle with all the sinners in the world that day. John declares: "And I saw the beast, and the kings of the earth, and their armies, gathered together to make war against him that sat on the horse, and against his army" (Revelation 19:19).

Heaven will win the battle. The slaughter will be great. In response to the invitation of an angel, the fowls of the earth will fill themselves with the flesh of the dead.

8

Israel—Going Home Again

ROMANS 11:1-29

Six Days of History

The fighting was fierce but short-lived. The war lasted only 6 days. Arabs and Jews struggled over land, the ownership of which had long been in question. Israel took territory she had not controlled for nearly 3,000 years. This area included the old part of the ancient city of Jerusalem. Within its sacred walls stood the Muslim shrine, the Dome of the Rock, on the site of Israel's historic temples.

Interest in the military events in the tiny land of Palestine was immediate and worldwide. It was the second war since 1948 when the Jews had returned to their homeland to become a nation again.

Faraway in America, a pretty little 8-year-old Sunday school girl asked her grandmother, "Does the Bible say Jesus will come when the Jews take Jerusalem again?" A lady inquired of a woman in the church, "Will Jesus return to earth again before the Battle of Armageddon?" Sincerely puzzled, an unsaved man approached a Christian gentleman and asked, "What does all this talk of Israel and Biblical prophecy mean?"

They Went to See

Some years later, the little Sunday school girl's pastor traveled abroad with a tour group. The party landed on the Island of Cyprus in the Mediterranean Sea as a final stop on its way to the Holy Land. As the people changed planes for the last leg of their journey, they realized the plane they were boarding stood apart from all the rest at the airport. It was guarded by Israeli soldiers carrying automatic weapons at their side.

After a short flight, the group's plane came to a stop at an airport in the Promised Land. All the passengers sat in silence for a few moments. Then three armed Israeli servicemen boarded the plane. One stood at each end of the passenger section, while the third circulated among the tourists and asked them official questions.

Finally, the passengers were allowed to leave the plane, but only two at a time. Once outside, they saw that the area was well guarded, and they learned that only recently a terrorist group had attacked such a planeload of people at that very airport and had killed several of them.

As they traveled through the Holy Land, along the highways the party saw the ruins of military vehicles that had been destroyed during the Six-Day War. They had purposely been left there as monuments of the conflict.

Finally, the group arrived in the capital city. The buses turned a corner to enter the walls of ancient Jerusalem. Just outside St. Stephen's Gate, scaffolding stood along the sides of a building that had been damaged by gunfire during the war.

Several more years have passed since the conflict, but the world still wonders about the significance of the Six-Day War. Will the Jews keep all or part of the territory they took? What will be the fate of the ancient city of Jerusalem and its sacred shrines?

The Times of the Gentiles

Characteristically, the Bible does not answer all the questions concerning the meaning of important current events. However, it does have much to say about the Israeli return to the Holy Land in the last days. Furthermore, it deals specifically with the conflict of the Jews and Gentiles over the control of Jerusalem.

Scripture speaks of the period when the nations dominate the City of Peace as the "times of the Gentiles" (Luke 21:24). There seems, then, to be political significance here for world affairs. In addition, a kindred reference by Paul to the "fulness of the Gentiles" appears to have spiritual significance for global evangelism (Romans 11:25).

A Matter of Priority

The Early Church gave priority to Jewish evangelism. This was also true of Jesus' earthly ministry. He indicated to the Syrophoenician woman that in His ministry He must give attention first to the Jews (Mark 7:24-30). Since they were the children of the Abrahamic Covenant, they must be given first chance at the gospel. However, the fact that Jesus answered her petition and healed her daughter shows that His priority of Jewish evangelism did not exclude Gentiles.

When the Lord sent out the Twelve He required the same priority of them. He instructed them: "Go not into the way of the Gentiles, and into any city

75

of the Samaritans enter ye not: but go rather to the lost sheep of the house of Israel" (Matthew 10:5,6). True, these restrictions were temporary, for later Jesus told His ministers to go into all the world to preach the gospel (Acts 1:8). They do, however, show an initial priority of Jewish evangelism.

Peter's early ministry followed the Master's instructions. Noting that they were children of the Covenant, he declared to a Jewish audience: "Unto you first God, having raised up his Son Jesus, sent him to bless you, in turning away every one of you from his iniquities" (Acts 3:26).

Paul followed this rule as a missionary. He always went first to the Jews. To a Jewish crowd, he said:

> It was necessary that the word of God should first have been spoken to you: but seeing ye put it from you, and judge yourselves unworthy of everlasting life, lo, we turn to the Gentiles (Acts 13:46).

The situation, then, is clear. At first the Church gave priority to Jewish evangelism because of God's covenant relationship with them. However, this does not mean Gentiles were excluded from grace. Such was never true, even in the Old Testament. God simply dealt specifically, although not exclusively, with the seed of Israel for a time.

Proceeding With Purpose

But the day came when God's purpose called for His dealing specifically, but not exclusively, with the Gentiles in global evangelism. The Church discovered this at the council in Jerusalem (Acts 15:13-17). After hearing Peter tell of Gentile conversions, James recognized that the Lord apparently intended "to take out of them a people for his name." He noted that the prophet Amos had spoken of a time when the Gentiles also would be called by the name of the Lord (Amos 9:11,12).

The discovery of God's plan to evangelize the Gentiles astonished the Jews (Acts 10:45; 11:18). That the Lord had "opened the door of faith unto the Gentiles" amazed them (Acts 14:27).

On the other hand, the Gentiles were naturally very glad to know the truth of God's love for them. In an address to them on one occasion, Paul credited Isaiah with predicting that the Messiah would bless not only the Jews but also the Gentiles (Isaiah 49:6). Luke comments: "And when the Gentiles heard this, they were glad, and glorified the word of the Lord" (Acts 13:48).

However, Paul also states that God's purpose will one day again require a priority of Jewish evangelism. He notes that at present the Jews generally are blinded by unbelief. He recognizes, of course, that this is not true of every Jew, for God always deals in the final analysis with people as individuals and not as ethnic groups. Thus, Paul says a remnant of Israel is presently being saved (Romans 11:5).

But, when "the fulness of the Gentiles be come in," the Lord will once more turn to the Jews, "and so all Israel shall be saved" (Romans 11:25,26). Then He will establish with them the new covenant He had promised through the prophets. Its one condition is that they believe on Jesus.

Gentile Christians are now recipients of the new covenant blessing because they have already met its conditions. And individual Gentiles may continue to share its grace even after the priority of world evangelism once more turns to the Jews.

Spiritual Israel

Contrary to all of this, some say the Church has now replaced Israel in the plan of God. Thus, He is finished with the Jews as an ethnic group. All prophecies and promises pertaining to them as a people must now be applied to the Church.

Scripture passages used in support of this position include Paul's declaration: "For they are not all Israel, which are of Israel" (Romans 9:6). Paul also states that "he is not a Jew, which is one outwardly," but rather "he is a Jew, which is one inwardly" (Romans 2:28,29). The implication is clear that there is a sense in which Christians, both Jew and Gentile, constitute "spiritual Israel."

However, although Paul teaches this truth, he is careful to show that God is still in a covenant relationship with the Jews as an ethnic group. It is in this frame of reference that he writes: "I say then, Hath God cast away his people? God forbid" (Romans 11:1). To ignore Paul's words and to say the Church is now, in every sense, the Israel of God is to be guilty of an allegorical rather than literal interpretation of Scripture.

Following his declaration, Paul spends a whole chapter discussing the relationship of natural Israel to God both at present and in the future. The Jews are the original branches of an olive tree that were broken off because of unbelief. When they recognize Jesus as their Messiah, through faith they will be grafted into the tree again.

At present, the Jews generally are blinded by unbelief. But one day their eyes will be opened, and "all Israel shall be saved" (Romans 11:26). Of course, they will be saved as individuals, not as a group, and because they each accept Christ, rather than simply because they are Jews.

World Politics

In addition to the religious significance of "the times of the Gentiles," there is also political significance for world affairs. Jesus said: "Jerusalem shall be trodden down of the Gentiles, until the times of the Gentiles be fulfilled" (Luke 21:24). At that moment, Jesus was predicting the fall of the city to the Romans. His prophecy was fulfilled in A.D. 70, beginning that period of Gentile control.

But the problem of sovereignty for the nation of Israel extends back well into Old Testament times. Ezekiel spoke dramatically of its loss in his day:

> Thus saith the Lord GOD; Remove the diadem, and take off the crown: this shall not be the same: exalt him that is low, and abase him that is high. I will overturn, overturn, overturn it: and it shall be no more, until he come whose right it is; and I will give it him (Ezekiel 21:26,27).

Thus, Ezekiel predicted the fall of the nation of Judah and the loss of its king. But he also indicated a new day in the future when the Jews will once more be sovereign and enjoy the reign of a righteous King.

Hosea gave a similar message. He declared: "For the children of Israel shall abide many days without a king, and without a prince," but "afterward shall the children of Israel return, and seek the LORD their God, and David their king; and shall fear the LORD and his goodness in the latter days" (Hosea 3:4,5).

79

Their words came true when the country fell to the Babylonians in 586 B.C. Although from time to time they were permitted to exercise varying degrees of self-government, the Jews were subservient to other nations until 1948. It is a marvel beyond words that in that year Israel became a nation again, as foretold in Scripture.

A Place to Live

Furthermore, the issue of Gentile occupation of the Holy Land has existed since the Jews lost their homeland to the Assyrians and Babylonians in Old Testament times. Even Moses said that sin would separate the Jews from the Promised Land (Deuteronomy 28:64-67). Graphically describing it, he declared: "And the LORD shall scatter thee among all people, from the one end of the earth even unto the other" (v. 64). But Moses also promised that repentance would bring a return to their homeland:

> Then the LORD thy God will turn thy captivity, and have compassion upon thee, and will return and gather thee from all the nations, whither the LORD thy God hath scattered thee (Deuteronomy 30:3).

True, both the dispersion and regathering of the Jews happened in the Old Testament. But the promise that they would be sovereign and have a king again has not yet been fulfilled.

Jesus spoke of another scattering for Israel following His day (Luke 21:24). Isaiah predicted that in the last days the Lord would once again gather His people in the Promised Land (Isaiah 11:11,12). Jesus also indicated the Jews would once more occupy Jerusalem when the times of the

Gentiles is fulfilled (Luke 21:24). Interestingly, the United Nations did not grant Israel the old part of the city in 1948. But Israel regained control of it later during the Six-Day War.

What's Ahead?

Did the "times of the Gentiles" end at that time? Has its political significance been realized? The world still debates the issue of the permanent control of "occupied Jerusalem." Will the Jews be allowed to keep it? Among proposed solutions to the problem is the suggestion that it be made an international city.

What does the Bible indicate will be the outcome of all this? Israel will remain in the center of world politics. John reveals that even after the Jews have regained control of Jerusalem and rebuilt the temple, Gentiles will be allowed once more to occupy the city. Of Jerusalem, he writes: "For it is given unto the Gentiles: and the holy city shall they tread under foot forty and two months" (Revelation 11:2).

No doubt it will be in such an hour when Israel's case seems hopeless that its people will lose confidence in self-sufficiency and turn anew to God. The final answer to their prayers will bring their Messiah back to earth to save the nation from annihilation at the hand of the Antichrist and the armies of the nations of the world.

The political significance of the "times of the Gentiles" and the spiritual significance of the "fulness of the Gentiles" are inseparably inter-related. The conversion of the Jews and their permanent possession of Jerusalem will occur together.

9

Christ's Rule of Righteousness

REVELATION 20:1-6

Diamonds in the Rough

The vacationing family of four set out to visit the only diamond mine in North America. Father, mother, son, and daughter traveled several miles to the site of the mine in southwest Arkansas.

They had it on good authority that anyone could search for diamonds at the site. It was no longer economically feasible to operate the mine commercially, so its owners had opened it to the public. Their income was the fees charged for the privilege of digging for the precious gems.

The vacationers arrived at the entrance to the mine. In a small office at the gate, the operators displayed a few diamonds that had been discovered at the site over a period of years.

But when they looked beyond the entrance, the family saw only what looked like people digging potatoes in an ordinary garden. A farm tractor plowed the field, while the unpaid miners scratched in the dirt behind it, hoping to discover that once-in-a-lifetime treasure. The right find would make them rich forever. What a dreamworld they could live in for the rest of their lives! They would have found their "pot of gold at the end of a rainbow" in a potato patch!

Happy Hunting Ground

After considering the charge for the privilege of searching for the diamonds, the small chance of finding any, and the discomforts of digging in the dirt on a hot summer day, the vacationing family decided to look for a different kind of treasure nearby. They learned of the Caddo Indians' burial grounds located a few miles from the diamond mine. A visit there would provide priceless information about a proud people of the past.

The ruins of the Caddo community suggested much about the living conditions of the native Americans who had occupied the site long ago. The burial grounds spoke particularly of the beliefs of the Indians.

Unlike some American Indians, the Caddo people buried their dead beneath the ground rather than in mounds above the earth. Uncovered grave sites indicated clearly that the natives believed in life after death. Apparently they thought the dead must have company in the next life. It appeared that an older person who died of natural causes was buried with younger ones at his side. Perhaps they were killed and buried with him expressly to provide companionship in the new world.

Items occupying the graves of the dead were apparently intended to serve as necessary utensils in the life after death. The Caddo, like most Indians, also buried weapons with their departed loved ones. These would be needed in the "happy hunting ground" to which they went.

Paradise Island

It seems, then, that there is a universal tendency among men to look for a perfect place in a land beyond tomorrow. Some dream of finding their "pot of gold at the end of the rainbow" in this life. For centuries, philosophers have described various utopias they have proposed for man on earth. In their imaginary world, all would be perfect politically, economically, and socially. At the same time, the American Indian hoped for his utopia in the world to come after death.

But God's Word holds true promise of a perfect place in the future for those who seek it through Jesus. By faith, they will have what others fail to find through their own works. This wonderful world ahead for believers includes more than just the heaven men hear so much about. Before followers of Jesus enjoy heaven eternally, God has planned for them a return to the conditions of the Garden of Eden right here on earth.

For 1,000 years, Jesus will reign in righteousness as King of kings while this world still stands. This fact is well established in Scripture. The Bible also describes the conditions on earth during this period and includes hints as to God's purpose in providing such a paradise for men on this planet.

Fact-finding Mission

The fact of an earthly reign of Jesus is well documented in the Bible. Actually, the Old Testament emphasized it to such an extent that the disciples of Jesus thought only of His earthly kingdom.

As Jews, Jesus' followers knew of the image in Nebuchadnezzar's dream (Daniel 2:31-45). They had heard of the stone that smote the image's feet, causing it to become as chaff and blow away, while the rock became a great mountain and filled the whole earth. They knew the stone represented the Messiah. In the last days, He would destroy the governments of the earth, as indicated by the 10 toes of the image. They remembered the words of the prophet: "And in the days of these kings shall the God of heaven set up a kingdom, which shall never be destroyed" (Daniel 2:44).

Consequently, Jesus' disciples repeatedly spoke to Him of His earthly rule. More than once they inquired as to the particular political assignments each would have in the kingdom. James and John went so far as to ask for the most prominent positions (Mark 10:35-45).

The disciples were so anxious for Jesus to break the yoke of Rome, restore national sovereignty to Israel, and set up His earthly kingdom that their thoughts were too political. To point them to the Kingdom's spiritual aspects, the Master had to say, "The kingdom of God is within you" (Luke 17:21). On another occasion He told them, "My kingdom is not of this world" (John 18:36).

However, in these remarks, the Lord does not negate the extensive scriptural predictions of an earthly messianic Kingdom. The disciples erred and needed to think of the spiritual more than the political aspects of God's rule on earth. They also were mistaken as to the time for establishing the earthly Kingdom. They were not as yet aware that it was related to Christ's second, rather than His first, coming to this world.

Therefore, just before the Ascension, the disciples asked, "Wilt thou at this time restore again the kingdom to Israel?" (Acts 1:6). The Master's response dealt only with their wrong view as to placing dates on God's prophetic calendar. If they had been mistaken in looking for an earthly Kingdom, this would have been the ideal time for Jesus to correct them.

Jesus' followers soon learned that His rule on earth would be established at His second coming.

Opinions of Men

In the years since, men have held varying views concerning Christ's earthly reign. They include premillennial, postmillennial, and amillennial positions. The postmillennial view teaches that ever-increasing conversions through the preaching of the gospel will gradually produce perfect conditions on earth. Once utopia has thus been achieved, it will last 1,000 years. Then Christ will return to earth to institute the eternal age.

But, one wonders how this can be since Paul says, "Evil men and seducers shall wax worse and worse" (2 Timothy 3:13). He further indicates that Jesus will return in "perilous" rather than perfect times (2 Timothy 3:1). The tragedies of World War II so thoroughly taught men that things are not getting better and better that the postmillennial view has all but been abandoned.

Amillennialism simply declares there will be no Millennium. Proponents of this view believe the reference to 1,000 years in Revelation 20:1-6 should not be taken literally. The figure is only symbolic and speaks of an indefinite period of time. This position has its roots in an allegorical method of interpreting the Bible. Origen, who lived in the third century, was among the first to suggest it.

But Augustine (of the fourth century) is the most often quoted source for amillennialists. He declared that although he had once believed in a literal reign of Christ on earth, he had changed his mind after concluding the Church is now "spiritual Israel."

Following Augustine, amillennialists say since Israel is now a "spiritual" term, all items in the only Biblical passage mentioning a 1,000-year period (Revelation 20:1-6) must be interpreted as symbolic rather than literal. Thus, Satan was "bound" figuratively at Calvary. He will not be bound literally at some future date. Disembodied saints in heaven now reign with Christ in a spiritual sense. They will never share a political reign with Him on earth. John's reference in the passage to a first resurrection speaks of the new birth. Thus, at conversion believers begin to reign with Jesus on earth, but only in a spiritual sense.

Yet strangely, amillennialists say John's reference to the second resurrection should be taken literally. There will be an actual bodily resurrection of all the dead at some future date. But how can one say the first resurrection is spiritual while the second is literal, and still maintain any consistency in his method of interpreting Scripture?

Amillennialists further reject the idea of a literal 1,000-year reign of Christ on earth because the figure appears in only one passage of Scripture, although listed there six times (Revelation 20:1-6). But would those of Jesus' day have been correct in refusing to believe in His virgin birth because it was specifically predicted only once in the Old Testament (Isaiah 7:14)?

A Sprout off the Old Stump

The fact is, however, those who hold a premillennial view have much more than just one passage on which to base their faith. God made promises to Abraham, Isaac, Jacob, and David, not all of which have been fulfilled as yet. He promised David a descendant on his throne, and the promise was such that only Jesus' reign over a political kingdom on earth could fulfill it. Obviously, this prophecy was not fulfilled by Christ's first coming.

The Old Testament foretold a terrible blow to David's dynasty which would be like the fatal cutting down of a tree. But a new sprout would spring up from the old stump. In the words of Isaiah: "There shall come forth a rod out of the stem of Jesse, and a Branch shall grow out of his roots" (Isaiah 11:1).

David's dynasty was cut down by the Babylonian captivity, and there has not been a descendant of David on his throne since then. Israel returned to the Promised Land, but they have never again had a king. Isaiah says they will return a "second time" and the "root of Jesse" will reign over them (Isaiah 11:10-12). His will be a righteous rule such as the Jews never knew under any Old Testament king (Isaiah 11:2-9).

All Is Well

To keep these promises to David, John says Jesus will come again. His return will signal the beginning of 1,000 years of righteous rule on earth, as suggested by the term *premillennial*. Those taking this position believe nothing short of a literal interpretation of the many millennial passages, including the one from John's pen, will do.

The Messiah will make universal righteousness possible, in part, by binding Satan at the very beginning of the 1,000 years (Revelation 20:1-6). Then Jesus will remain present on earth personally to sit as King and Governor of the nations (Zechariah 14:9). Genuine justice will be possible because His decisions will stem from divine attributes (Isaiah 11:2-5). The result will be universal peace (Micah 4:3,4). Men will study war no more.

The saints will share the Messiah's righteous rule. According to John, they will sit on various administrative thrones (Revelation 20:1-6). Jesus also promised this (Matthew 19:28).

Creation will experience a new birth (Romans 8:19-22). The curse of Genesis 3:17-19 will be lifted (Revelation 22:3). The nature of animals will be changed from ferocious back to their original state (Isaiah 11:6-9). The lion and lamb will lie peacefully side by side. Sickness will decrease, and long life will return to man (Isaiah 65:20).

Things will also change in the religious realm. The knowledge of the Lord will be universal (Isaiah 11:9). Jews will experience the "know-so" salvation of the new covenant (Jeremiah 31:31-34). Born-again Christians already have its benefits because they have met its conditions by believing on Jesus (Hebrews 8:6-13).

Since Israel will finally accept their Messiah, God will pour His Spirit wondrously on them (Joel 2:28,29). This outpouring began at Pentecost and has continued to be experienced by those who believe (Acts 2:14-21). Gentiles will join Jews in devotion to the Lord. Worship will be worldwide (Zechariah 8:20-23).

Some chide premillennialists for combining

Scripture passages from various parts of the Bible when drawing their conclusions on conditions during Christ's earthly reign. However, Paul's method of handling Scripture justifies this procedure. For example, he cites passages from Genesis and Psalms in support of his doctrine of justification by faith (Romans 4:1-8).

Reason Enough

Some may ask: "Why would God want to continue working with men on earth when this present age ends? Hasn't He already completed His program for the Jews?"

But one must accept the ways of God as explained in the Bible whether or not they appear reasonable. He must not try to "explain them away" by making literal statements into figurative ones or vice versa. Rather, he must treat the language of the Bible much as he does any speech, accepting it in its general and ordinary sense.

Still, there seems to be reason enough for the Lord's plans for a Millennium. Perhaps the Millennium will be God's way of providing a time of bliss on earth as a sort of first step toward that of heaven. Also, He may wish to provide man with one last test under ideal conditions before Judgment Day. Some say a perfect environment produces perfect men. The Millennium will disprove that (Revelation 20:7-9).

Basically, however, the Millennium will be required to complete the conditions of the covenants God has made with Israel. In speaking of the certainty of the Lord's promises to them, Paul assures all that "the gifts and calling of God are without repentance" (Romans 11:29).

10

The World to Come

2 PETER 3:7-14

Fire in the Sky

The setting of the sun and the shadows of the evening brought welcome relief from the summer heat for the farmers of a rural community in the southland. The economic difficulties of the Depression days demanded long, hard hours of work in the fields.

With the chores completed and supper over, teenagers from the various families headed down the dusty road to celebrate the birthday of a friend. Such social diversions helped break the monotony of those confining years.

After the party ended, a group of the young people walked leisurely toward their homes. Laughter was much the order of the day. It was a moment of good times among the bad.

Suddenly, the darkness of the night was broken by a strange brightness in the northern sky. It seemed as if the heavens were on fire! An indescribable soberness immediately settled on all present. In a recent "brush arbor" meeting, the young people had heard an evangelist speak about the coming end of the world. Was the fiery sky the beginning of the end? The youths rushed to their homes and called their parents outside to see the strange sight. Serious discussions and some prayer followed.

What the teenagers had seen, of course, was the northern lights. Scientists say the phenomenon occurs when protons and electrons shoot out from the sun and strike the earth's upper atmosphere. Various charged particles then glow much like those of a fluorescent light bulb, which results in the spectacular display of red and green colors in the sky.

The country preacher had been entirely correct in warning that rural community of the end of the world. The Bible speaks clearly of the end of the present order of things. However, the real "end of the world" will come at the end of Christ's earthly kingdom, when His millennial reign concludes. It will bring the beginning of the eternal heavenly Kingdom.

Basis in Fact

The original basis for discussion about the end of the world is a statement Jesus made just before He ascended to heaven. To the disciples who stood wondering at His imminent departure, Jesus said: "I am with you alway, even unto the end of the world" (Matthew 28:20).

However, at that time the Lord was not speaking of the end of the planet earth. Rather, He had in mind what the Greek indicates literally as the "end of the age." In other words, He was referring to the consummation of the present order of things. The plan of God for the present dispensation, or period of grace, will one day be finished. The end of the period will come at the time of the return of Christ to earth, at His revelation to all men. Therefore, in essence, Jesus was saying to His followers: "Visibly I go away, but spiritually I am with you yet, right down to the time of the end of this age when I will come again to the earth."

It is clear, then, that what men usually think of when they hear the "end of the world" mentioned is based on other passages of Scripture. For example, Peter says:

> But the day of the Lord will come as a thief in the night; in the which the heavens shall pass away with a great noise, and the elements shall melt with fervent heat, the earth also and the works that are therein shall be burned up (2 Peter 3:10).

The Psalmist also speaks of the end of planet earth. Referring to the heavens and the earth, he says they "shall wax old like a garment" (Psalm 102:26). Accordingly, the Lord will change them as one changes worn out clothing. Then the Psalmist declares plainly, "They shall perish." The writer of the Book of Hebrews repeats these words to a New Testament audience (Hebrews 1:10-12). And Isaiah writes: "The heavens shall vanish away like smoke, and the earth shall wax old like a garment" (Isaiah 51:6).

These statements are among the most sobering in Scripture. Men have pondered their meaning for centuries. Although God does not need natural phenomenon to complete His work, the coming of the atomic age has made the literal fulfillment of these prophecies appear much more possible. The fact that some think the events referred to will renovate rather than annihilate the earth does not weaken the magnitude of the coming catastrophe.

Firm Footing

Although words like Peter's were not meant merely to frighten men, they were intended to have a sobering effect even on believers. Appropriately Peter says: "Seeing then that all these things shall be dissolved, what manner of persons ought ye to be in all holy conversation and godliness ... ?" (2 Peter 3:11,12). Then he adds a reassuring note: "Nevertheless we, according to his promise, look for new heavens and a new earth, wherein dwelleth righteousness" (v. 13).

A prophetic utterance of Haggai with a similar purpose came long ago. Through him the Lord said: "Yet once, it is a little while, and I will shake the heavens, and the earth, and the sea, and the dry land" (Haggai 2:6). Recalling this, the writer of Hebrews says the prophecy "signifieth the removing of those things that are shaken, as of things that are made, that those things which cannot be shaken may remain" (Hebrews 12:27).

Man is prone to think the earth beneath him is the most dependable thing in life. As long as his feet are on the good old solid ground he is safe. Nothing drastic can happen here. But the Bible declares that this planet is no permanent foundation on which to build. Only Jesus offers a place to stand where things will never be shaken but ever remain.

Sin's Final Struggle

Apparently, then, the close of the Millennium will bring to an end God's purposes for mother earth, at least in its present form. But before the end of the world, sin will exert one final struggle.

Satan will be bound for the 1,000 years of Christ's rule, but after that, John says:

> He must be loosed a little season .... And when the thousand years are expired, Satan shall be loosed out of his prison, and shall go out to deceive the nations (Revelation 20:3,7,8).

Moreover, the Lord will show that the depraved nature of man is not altered by a perfect environment. After 1,000 years of bliss, men, numbered as the sands of the sea, will follow Satan in this final rebellion against God.

John says: "They ... compassed the camp of the saints about, and the beloved city: and fire came down from God out of heaven, and devoured them" (Revelation 20:9). Immediately, instead of being returned to prison, the devil will be cast into the lake of fire and brimstone. There he, his angels, and all his followers will be "tormented day and night for ever and ever" (Revelation 20:10).

Surrender of Sovereignty

At this point in time, the earthly part of God's plan of redemption will be at an end. Christ will have demonstrated that neither punishment nor peace will save sinful human nature. He will have shown that sin's only cure is through the Cross. Death will have been defeated, first at His resurrection and then by the resurrection of all His servants. All earthly authority will have been put down at the beginning of His earthly reign. With Satan's confinement to hell, Christ will have subdued the last of all powers of rebellion in the universe. Then He will be ready to surrender the commission that brought His earthly assignment to Him. Speaking of this, Paul says:

> Then cometh the end, when he shall have delivered up the kingdom to God, even the Father; when he shall have put down all rule, and all authority and power. For he must reign, till he hath put all enemies under his feet. The last enemy that shall be destroyed is death (1 Corinthians 15:24-26).

When He has surrendered His earthly sovereignty, Christ will return to His preincarnate place in the Godhead. As Paul writes: "And when all things shall be subdued unto him, then shall the Son also himself be subject unto him that put all things under him, that God may be all in all" (1 Corinthians 15:28).

World Without End

At the same time that Peter predicted the end of this world, he immediately promised new heavens and a new earth (2 Peter 3:10-13). In like manner, John writes: "And I saw a new heaven and a new earth: for the first heaven and the first earth were passed away" (Revelation 21:1). Through Isaiah, Jehovah declares: "Behold, I create new heavens and a new earth: and the former shall not be remembered, nor come into mind" (Isaiah 65:17). This will signal the beginning of that "world without end" of which Paul speaks (Ephesians 3:21). Things of time will be swallowed up in eternity.

Columbus claimed God had told him to go find the new earth promised in the Book of Revelation and had given him an indication of where it was. But it is obvious that in coming to America he didn't find a perfect world. The Lord has that yet in store for His servants.

The prospects of a better world in the eternal age meant much to John. Suffering, persecuted, and banished to the Island of Patmos for preaching the gospel, he must have been greatly encouraged by his vision of a new heaven and a new earth. One of the first things about the new world that attracted his attention was that "there was no more sea" (Revelation 21:1). At the time, John was surrounded by the Mediterranean Sea. The fact that the new earth will contain no oceans of water, the symbol of separation and turbulence, must have been very comforting to him.

The eternal age will bring an end to all earth's miseries. Earlier, the Holy Spirit, through John, promised that God the Father will wipe all tears from the eyes of His children (Revelation 7:17). Now He adds the good news that there will never be an occasion for any new tears. He declares:

> And God shall wipe away all tears from their eyes; and there shall be no more death, neither sorrow, nor crying, neither shall there be any more pain: for the former things are passed away (Revelation 21:4).

As wonderful as all this is, the greatest blessing of the new world is that it will bring the eternal presence of God to His followers. John writes:

> Behold, the tabernacle of God is with men, and he shall dwell with them, and they shall be his people, and God himself shall be with them, and be their God (Revelation 21:3).

This is exactly the opposite of the fate of unbelievers. They will be banished forever from the presence of the Lord. Paul speaks of sinners as those "who shall be punished with everlasting destruction from the presence of the Lord, and from the glory of his power" (2 Thessalonians 1:9).

Heaven Come Down

A beautiful city will serve as the capital in the eternal kingdom of God. John depicts the New Jerusalem as a city coming down from heaven like a bride adorned for her husband.

In John's vision, an angel measures the city and finds it to be "foursquare" (Revelation 21:16). It is 1,500 miles in length, breadth, and height. Its walls are "great and high." Entrance into the city is through 12 gates, each made of pearl, and the names of the 12 sons of Jacob are written on the gates. The walls of the city are decked with all kinds of jewels and precious stones, and its streets are of gold.

As the seat of government, the New Jerusalem will house the throne of God. John saw a marvel associated with it. Speaking of the angel who guided him in his vision, he says: "And he showed me a pure river of water of life, clear as crystal, proceeding out of the throne of God and of the Lamb" (Revelation 22:1). Waters from this river nourish the tree of life. The tree bears 12 kinds of fruit, one for each month of the year, and its leaves are for "the healing of the nations" (Revelation 22:2).

Darkness will be no more in the eternal abode of the righteous. John declares:

And there shall be no night there; and they need no candle, neither light of the sun; for the Lord God giveth them light: and they shall reign for ever and ever (Revelation 22:5).

It's Enough

Generally, when men think of going to heaven it is this eternal age that they have in mind. News of such a wonderful place where the redeemed will be forever stirs the deepest hopes within man. Yet, he recognizes that there are mysteries associated with it. The Lord has revealed just enough about it to make man want to know more.

The fact is, though, the further one goes in a study of God's timetable of the future, the less he finds revealed. Sacred writers record much about the second coming of Christ. They pen a considerable amount on the Antichrist and the Tribulation period. They give less detail, however, about the Millennium, the golden age to come. And the least amount of material is given about the eternal age following the Millennium. Like prophecy in general, one must confess that heaven has its mysteries.

Yet, God has revealed enough. Only an unwholesome curiosity demands more. Obviously, if man could have profited, the Lord would have opened the door of the future wider. No doubt He wishes men to keep their eyes on Him as the God of the future, rather than focusing on the material aspects of heaven.

Near the end of his vision, John was ready to worship the angel who told him of the glories of the world to come. But the angel stopped him, saying, "Worship God" (Revelation 22:9).

11

What Happens When a Person Dies?

2 CORINTHIANS 5:1-10

Where to From Here?

On a perfectly beautiful spring afternoon, two
couples neared the site of a picturesque monastery.
They turned off the highway to travel a narrow
unpaved road leading to the community of monks.
On top of one of the highest hills in the area, they
stopped for a breathtaking view of the brothers'
housing quarters, which stood about a mile away
across the valley. The quaint dormitory and the
simple chapel of the devout Catholic group were
clearly visible on that cloudless spring day.

For a moment, the couples felt as if they were in
the Swiss Alps—without having to fly the many
miles to reach that distant land. Slowly, they continued their journey toward the buildings. They
didn't want to miss even a moment of this opportunity to enjoy the beauty surrounding them. Not
far from the monks' quarters, they crossed the low-
water bridge that spanned a clear mountain
stream. A short distance away was the long,
swinging footbridge the brothers used when the
creek flooded. The trip ended in the parking lot, in
the quietness found only in such places of solitude.

After being graciously received at the guest house, the two male members of the party received a tour of the monastery. During the rounds, they engaged in serious conversation with their guide, a monk of many years.

One man asked, "Do you expect to go straight to heaven when you die?" The monk's quick reply was, "Oh no. Very few are good enough for that."

The comments that followed centered on possible scriptural support for teachings on purgatory. With no real evidence from the Bible, the monk sought help from church tradition. He said he had read of a pious lady who lived centuries ago and had the ability to tell where souls went at death. He continued, "Of the thousands of spirits she saw leaving bodies in death, only a half dozen went straight to heaven. The rest went either to purgatory or hell."

This incident indicates the interest people have in the subject of life after death. Many false views about where the soul goes when a person dies have been suggested, but the Bible contains the only acceptable view. Although the Old Testament gives some insights, what God has chosen to say on the subject is clearest in the New Testament.

Purifying Fire

The general teachings of Scripture show that a person does not go immediately to his permanent abode at death. This is true for both saint and sinner.

If the Christian receives the fullness of everlasting blessing the moment he dies, what is the purpose of the resurrection? Likewise, if the unbeliever receives his full punishment at death, what is the need of a later judgment for him? This is not to say, of course, that the intermediate state, the period between death and resurrection, is not wonderful for the believer and awful for the sinner.

Granting, then, that there is an intermediate state for all the dead, what is it like? Among the false views is the one that reasons that almost everyone goes to a purging place at death. With careful prayers for them by the living and patience on their own part, the dead will be purified through the sufferings of purgatory.

Grasping for scriptural support, those who hold this view cite Jesus' statement that, in the life to come, men will have to account for even their idle words (Matthew 12:36,37). But, although Jesus discourages reckless use of the tongue, the Bible teaches that confession, faith, and grace bring cleansing from sin (1 John 1:7,9). One is saved by grace and not by works, neither in this world nor in the one to come.

Teachers of purgatory also say the Master spoke of a man owing a debt, failing to pay, being cast into a debtors' prison, and not getting out until he has paid the last cent (Matthew 5:25,26). But here the Lord was clearly discussing earthly relationships among men, rather than one's standing before God in the afterlife.

If one does not make things right with the Lord here, it will be too late in the world to come. There is no second chance in purgatory or elsewhere. A person will be judged by the things he did while he was "in his body" (2 Corinthians 5:10).

Rapping With Tables

Another false view concerning the intermediate

state says that the dead are in a place where the living may communicate with them. Those propagating this position recall Saul's talk with the deceased Samuel (1 Samuel 28:7-25). But the Bible says Saul died because he asked "counsel of one that had a familiar spirit, to inquire of it; and inquired not of the LORD" (1 Chronicles 10:13,14).

The Bible expressly forbids efforts to communicate with the dead (Deuteronomy 18:10-12). Necromancers, those who claim they talk with deceased persons, are said to be an abomination to God. Although they claim support from the Bible for their art, they reject most of the teachings of Scripture. Through table-tapping techniques, they report that the unbelieving dead are happy where they are, that there are no fires of hell there, and that in general all is well. The Bible paints a contrasting picture for those who reject Christ.

Asleep in Jesus

A third false view of the intermediate state says that the soul sleeps between death and the resurrection. They reason: Doesn't the Bible speak of saints as being asleep in the grave (Matthew 27:52)? Didn't Paul refer to dead Christians as being asleep (1 Thessalonians 4:13,14)? Didn't even Jesus say the dead Lazarus was merely asleep (John 11:11-14)?

True, but in these cases a euphemism was used. This is a figure of speech where a soft word is used to speak of a harsh event. The Master substituted the expression *sleep* to speak of Lazarus' *death*. But when His followers wrongly took His words as being literal, "then said Jesus unto them plainly, Lazarus is dead" (John 11:14).

103

Neither the saint's nor the sinner's soul sleeps in death. Consciousness does not end when the soul leaves the body. Regrettably, those who teach that souls sleep also say that only the righteous will awaken to a continued existence beyond the resurrection. All others will arise only to annihilation. The Bible, however, supports no such view.

Hell and the Grave

Some insights into the intermediate state appear in the Old Testament. The name given the place of departed spirits is *sheol.* The ancients viewed it as the immediate destiny of the dead.

What kind of place is it? In the Authorized Version, the Hebrew word *sheol* is translated in several ways. It is a pit (Job 17:16); it is hell (Psalm 9:17); and, in some places, it is even called the grave (Genesis 37:35). But these English words can hardly express the images called to the Hebrew mind by the term *sheol.* Certainly there is nothing in them to suggest that "hell is nothing but the grave," as some say.

When Jacob, at the supposed death of Joseph, said, "I will go down into the grave [*sheol*] unto my son mourning," he was not thinking of a hole in the ground. Rather, he was expressing his hope of seeing his son again in the world to come.

The ancient Jews often spoke of being "gathered to one's people" when life on earth ceased (Genesis 25:8; 49:33). David expressed the same hope at the death of his infant child: "I shall go to him, but he shall not return to me" (2 Samuel 12:23).

Job also declared a hope that departed spirits find the place of their confinement better than this world. He said:

> There the wicked cease from troubling; and there the weary be at rest. There the prisoners rest together; they hear not the voice of the oppressor. The small and great are there; and the servant is free from his master (Job 3:17-19).

Some wonder at the words of the writer of Ecclesiastes concerning *sheol*. He says: "For there is no work, nor device, nor knowledge, nor widsom, in the grave [*sheol*], whither thou goest" (Ecclesiastes 9:10). But one must remember that these are the remarks of a man who was away from God in an apostate condition. They express the skeptical pessimism of the unregenerate human mind, rather than the truth of God about the intermediate state.

Escape From Prison

Did the Hebrew servant of Jehovah ever expect his stay in *sheol* to end? Indeed he did, although naturally his understanding of the resurrection came short of that of New Testament times. Without a hope that the *sheol* experience would one day end, it would be incorrect even to speak of it as the abode of departed spirits in an intermediate state.

The Psalmist expected deliverance from *sheol*. He writes: "But God will redeem my soul from the power of the grave [*sheol*]: for he shall receive me" (Psalm 49:15). In another passage, David speaks clearly of his own resurrection as well as that of Jesus: "For thou wilt not leave my soul in hell [*sheol*]; neither wilt thou suffer thine Holy One to see corruption" (Psalm 16:10).

Hosea also hoped for deliverance from *sheol*. As the voice of Jehovah, he declares:

> I will ransom them from the power of the grave

105

[*sheol*]; I will redeem them from death: O death, I will be thy plagues; O grave [*sheol*], I will be thy destruction (Hosea 13:14).

Although he does not refer specifically to *sheol*, Job certainly manifested confidence in a personal resurrection. He exclaims:

And though after my skin worms destroy this body, yet in my flesh shall I see God: whom I shall see for myself, and mine eyes shall behold, and not another (Job 19:26,27).

Prison Torture

Although there are hints of it in the Old Testament, the New Testament speaks clearly of the intermediate state as being a very different experience for the saint and the sinner.

Peter describes what happened to rebellious angels during their period of probation. He says God "cast them down to hell, and delivered them into chains of darkness, to be reserved unto judgment" (2 Peter 2:4). As for sinful men, he goes on to indicate that in like manner the Lord will "reserve the unjust unto the day of judgment to be punished" (2 Peter 2:9).

Luke records Jesus' remarks about the rich man who went to hell at death (Luke 16:19-31). "Hell" here is translated from the Greek word *hades*. It is generally considered the equivalent of the Hebrew *sheol*. Interestingly, it is this hell (hades) that is finally cast into the lake of fire (Revelation 20:14). Again, then, hell can hardly be simply the grave. The prison house of the dead during the intermediate state, not the grave, will end up in the lake of fire.

The rich man's experiences are among the most

unpleasant in the universe. If his is the story of the intermediate state for sinners, it pictures something to be shunned—to say nothing of the "second death" to follow in the lake of fire.

Paradise Regained

In sharp contrast to the intermediate state of the unrighteous, the state of the righteous is one of bliss. For example, the rich man went to hades at death, while Lazarus went to "Abraham's bosom" (Luke 16:19-31). No place would be more desirable for a dying Jew. The rich man was "tormented," but poor Lazarus was "comforted."

The repentant thief dying on the cross at Jesus' side was promised a place in paradise that very day (Luke 23:43). The name *paradise* reminds one of conditions in the Garden of Eden before the fall of man. Paul says paradise is located in the "third heaven" (2 Corinthians 12:2-4). It is promised to all who keep following the Lord and overcome (Revelation 2:7).

The intermediate state for the righteous is a land of rest. John says the dead in Christ "rest from their labors" (Revelation 14:13). The Lord told the martyred ones who wondered how much longer they must wait for their full reward that they must "rest yet for a little season" (Revelation 6:11). But that rest is not one of inactivity. John indicates that the elders in heaven are "before the throne of God, and serve him day and night in his temple" (Revelation 7:15).

But whether resting or serving, according to Paul, things are "far better" for the Christian at the moment of death than the best this life has to offer (Philippians 1:23). The reason for this is that when a Christian dies he goes immediately to be "with the Lord." Paul considered it very desirable to be "absent from the body" so that he might be "present with the Lord" (2 Corinthians 5:1-9).

Continuous Communion

Death does not break the believer's fellowship with the Lord. Between death and the resurrection he is in continuous communion with Jesus. Paul declares plainly that death cannot separate the Christian from his Lord (Romans 8:38,39).

In his vision, John sees the souls of the martyrs living "under the altar," somewhere near the throne of God (Revelation 6:9-11). The Lord is close at hand. They talk with Him and ask, "How long, O Lord, holy and true, dost thou not judge and avenge our blood on them that dwell on the earth?" God responds to them and answers their question with words of love, comfort, and reassurance. The Lord also gives them a token of the full reward that awaits them at the resurrection and beyond. John writes: "And white robes were given unto every one of them" (Revelation 6:11).

Apart from the blessings of heaven for eternity, the continuous communion with the Lord between death and the resurrection makes the Christian life the one to choose. This is true in spite of the reproach, persecution, and suffering that following Jesus sometimes brings. Paul says: "For I reckon that the sufferings of this present time are not worthy to be compared with the glory which shall be revealed in us" (Romans 8:18).

12

The Court of No Appeal

REVELATION 20:11-15

Setting for Evangelism

For 2 weeks the pastor, evangelist, and people enjoyed a great time together in nightly meetings at the church. Saints found revival of spirit. Some sinners found salvation. But in the minds of all there was a great need nearby that could not be ignored.

A few miles away, the town that served as the seat of government for the county had no church where the full gospel was preached. The Christians of the church in revival were not content to simply enjoy the blessings and forget the hundreds of lost souls nearby. The pastor especially felt a great burden for that town. Something had to be done.

The minister asked the evangelist if he would consider remaining in the area for several more days to preach in the county seat. After receiving the preacher's consent to stay for the additional services, the pastor sought suitable quarters for the soul-winning effort.

County officials agreed to permit the use of the

courtroom for the meetings. Since the town was built around a square, with the courthouse in the center, this meant the gospel would literally be preached from the "heart" of the community. The courtroom was located on the second story of the building and occupied the whole floor. With all the windows open on those hot summer evenings, the people who stood on the grounds and those who sat on the benches below could hear the singing, testimonies, and preaching of the services.

Those who came inside for the meetings sat in the spectators' section of the courtroom. In front of them were the traditional 12 chairs for the jury. In the center was an ornate bench for the judge, and behind it was his vacant leather chair.

What a setting for evangelism! It was made to order—especially for the final night of the services when the evangelist spoke about Judgment Day. As the speaker talked of the day when men will stand before God as Judge, the somber atmosphere of the courtroom and its tangible items to which the speaker could refer contributed to the several conversions of the evening.

Justice Demands It

The very nature of things demands that there be a Judgment Day. Many crimes remain hidden and go unpunished in this life. For justice to prevail in the universe, they must one day be brought to light and each offender must suffer the penalty.

By the same token, many deeds of kindness remain unknown in this world and thus go by without commendation. These, too, must be publicly revealed and rewarded if God is just.

Paul wrote to Timothy about all this. Apparently the younger preacher was disturbed at the lack of justice in the world. The older minister told him:

> Some men's sins are open beforehand, going before to judgment; and some men they follow after. Likewise also the good works of some are manifest beforehand; and they that are otherwise cannot be hid (1 Timothy 5:24,25).

In other words, God finally will see that justice is done in the case of both good and evil in this life. The Bible teaches that all created intelligence, whether men or angels, will one day answer to God for deeds done in the body. This makes the subject of judgment one of the most practical of all prophetic teachings. Every person will give an account.

The fact that justice will prevail seems to be a necessary stimulant to encourage correct conduct in men during their journey on earth. The wise man of old observed: "Because sentence against an evil work is not executed speedily, therefore the heart of the sons of men is fully set in them to do evil" (Ecclesiastes 8:11). A modern statesman declared that what he dreads most for his country is not the day of judgment but the day of no judgment.

The One and the Many

A surface reading of some Scripture passages suggests the idea of one general judgment for all men at some future time. For example, Jesus said:

> The hour is coming, in the which all that are in the graves shall hear his voice, and shall come forth; they

that have done good, unto the resurrection of life; and they that have done evil, unto the resurrection of damnation (John 5:28,29).

Some think this implies a general judgment following a general resurrection. But other passages show there will not be a general resurrection for both good and evil. In fact, those resurrections will be separated by 1,000 years (Revelation 20:4-6).

Therefore, instead of one judgment for all, the Bible teaches several judgments of various kinds, depending on the needs of those who appear in the different courts. There will be a judgment for believers, one for angels, and still another for the wicked dead.

As the accused sometimes seeks a "change of venue," or a trial in a different court where greater prospects of a fair trial appear, so one may choose his court in accounting to God. When the Jews sought to rush Paul's case through to conviction in spite of lack of evidence, he said: "I appeal unto Caesar" (Acts 25:11). He concluded that there he would get a fairer trial.

Paul used his knowledge of Roman law and his rights under it as a citizen to his advantage. Likewise, a knowledge of the judgments can affect one's choices today and, therefore, his destiny tomorrow.

Believable Verdict

The judgments that affect the believer are three in number. The first of these concerns the judgment of his sins. Legally, the believer's sins were judged in Christ at the cross. Paul says God "made him to be sin for us, who knew no sin" (2 Corinthians 5:21). Literally, then, He took the believer's place in the judgment of his sins at Calvary.

It was there that Jesus potentially became the "Saviour of all men" (1 Timothy 4:10). He becomes their actual Saviour as they each believe individually. When one believes on Jesus, he may then say with Paul: "Christ hath redeemed us from the curse of the law, being made a curse for us: for it is written, Cursed is every one that hangeth on a tree" (Galatians 3:13).

Since the believer's sins were judged and punished at the Cross, obviously he will not be haled into court to account for them again. John records the Master's words: "He that heareth my word, and believeth on him that sent me, hath everlasting life, and shall not come into condemnation [or judgment]" (John 5:24).

The situation of the believer is similar to that of the accused in court. If he has been tried and declared not guilty, the "law of double jeopardy" forbids that he ever be tried again on the same charge.

The basis for the verdict in the judgment of the believer's sins includes the law of God, the righteousness of Christ, and the repenting sinner's attitude toward Jesus. God's law demands the death penalty for sin. The sinless Christ paid the debt. But for one to benefit, he must accept the unbelievable verdict of the Judge: "You are not guilty for Jesus' sake." John writes: "He that believeth on him is not condemned: but he that believeth not is condemned already" (John 3:18).

In another passage the apostle says: "He that believeth not God hath made him a liar; because he believeth not the record that God gave of his Son" (1 John 5:10). To call a fellow human a liar is among the worst offenses. But who would be so foolish as to defy God that way? No wonder that person stands "condemned already."

Self-evaluation

The truth concerning the judgment of the believer's sins should not lead him to a sense of false security. John's promise of not coming into judgment is related to an ongoing attitude of believing on Jesus.

Accordingly, there are other judgments the believer must consider. For one thing, as a son, in times of disobedience the Christian is judged and chastened by the Father (Hebrews 12:5-11). Then, too, the believer is told to judge himself so it will not be necessary for God to judge him (1 Corinthians 11:28-32). Paul says: "For if we would judge ourselves, we should not be judged." He writes later: "Examine yourselves, whether ye be in the faith; prove your own selves" (2 Corinthians 13:5).

In daily Bible study and prayer, and especially at the Communion table, the Christian must judge himself. He should examine both his motives and his conduct by the standards of God's law. When he finds failures, he must confess them and ask for grace to overcome them. John declares: "If we confess our sins, he is faithful and just to forgive us our sins, and to cleanse us from all unrighteousness" (1 John 1:9).

It is true that an unwholesome degree of self-accusation has negative effects. It fits into the sorrow of this world which works death (2 Corinthians 7:10). It can lead one to agree with the accuser of the brethren (Revelation 12:10).

However, self-evaluation as taught in Scripture produces desirable results. It affords a clear conscience toward God (1 John 3:20,21) and man (Acts 24:16). It brings freedom from the judgment of God (1 Corinthians 11:31). On the last day, it will give the Christian great confidence when he meets the Lord face to face (1 John 2:28).

Prize for Performance

The believer must also be judged for his performance in the area of Christian service. The court session for this is known as the Judgment Seat of Christ. Paul mentions it twice in his writings. He says: "For we must all appear before the judgment seat of Christ" (2 Corinthians 5:10). Writing again to Christians, he declares: "So then every one of us shall give account of himself to God" (Romans 14:12).

The judgment referred to here does not relate to one's salvation. Nor does it concern the correctness of one's conduct in this world. It deals only with the quality of the believer's works in serving God as a laborer in the vineyard.

The classic passage on the subject (1 Corinthians 3:7-15) actually discusses the kind of ministry preachers have. They may build using lasting materials such as gold, silver, or precious stones, or they may use wood, hay, or stubble. The fires of time, and especially of Judgment Day, will prove the quality of their work. Then, as Paul says: "Every man shall receive his own reward according to his own labor" (1 Corinthians 3:8).

Banquet Honors

What is true of preachers is true of every believer in the area of Christian service. Paul concludes:

> If any man's work abide which he hath built thereupon, he shall receive a reward. If any man's work shall be burned, he shall suffer loss (1 Corinthians 3:14-15).

The basis of this judgment concerns faithfulness and efficiency in service. Hearing Jesus' words, "Well done, thou good and faithful servant" (Matthew 25:21), will be a great part of the reward. But assignment for additional service will also be involved. The Master will also say: "Thou hast been faithful over a few things, I will make thee ruler over many."

In Jesus' parables on stewardship, the estate owner gives assignments "to every man according to his several ability" (Matthew 25:15). After returning from his long trip, the owner examines the servants on the basis of efficiency as well as faithfulness. He then distributes new assignments for service according to the degree of industry each steward has demonstrated in his original duty. One servant is put in charge of 10 cities and another is given the rule over five. But one is denied the opportunity of further managerial service (Luke 19:12-27).

Apparently, the Judgment Seat of Christ will convene at the Marriage Supper (Revelation 19:7-9). While the Tribulation rages on earth, Jesus will, as He promised, once again sit at a table with His own (Matthew 26:29). As at banquets on earth, Jesus will present honors and awards. He will also make assignments for future service in the Millennium (Revelation 20:4,6).

Angels in Trouble

Not only will men account to God, but angels will also give account. Jude says of the angels that sinned, God "hath reserved [them] in everlasting chains under darkness unto the judgment of the great day" (Jude 6). At the end of the Millennium, they will come to trial and Christians will sit as judges (1 Corinthians 6:3). It seems Satan, himself a fallen angel, will be among those judged. The intent of the trial will be to manifest rather than determine guilt. Jesus says everlasting fire is prepared for the devil and his angels (Matthew 25:41).

Final Item on the Agenda

The final judgment on the docket of heaven's court will be that of the wicked dead. This judgment is what men usually think of when they speak of "Judgment Day." More correctly, it is the Great White Throne Judgment.

John graphically describes the awesome scene (Revelation 20:11-15). God will sit as Judge of the universe. No doubt He will do so in the person of Jesus. Peter says Jesus "was ordained of God to be the Judge of quick and dead" (Acts 10:42). Paul concurs (Acts 17:31).

The subjects on trial here will be all the unsaved dead. In that hour, men will be judged on the basis of "those things which were written in the books" (Revelation 20:12)—apparently a record of their deeds. But, notice, the Judge will also consult the book of life. Only those who believe on Christ have their names recorded there. The real basis of judgment, then, will be what men have done with Jesus.

Solemnly, John states the result of the Great White Throne Judgment: "And whosoever was not found written in the book of life was cast into the lake of fire" (Revelation 20:15). This is the court of no appeal, and it will be in session at the end of the Millennium.

The good news is that one may still choose his court. He may come to the court of a repentant sinner and have his crimes attended to in the judgment of the believer's sins. Otherwise, his sins will be publicly exposed at the Great White Throne Judgment and eternal judgment will be pronounced.

13

Time Without End

LUKE 16:19-31

A Major Concern

The great day had finally arrived. The young man had graduated from high school and was now on the campus at State College, ready to begin his career as a scholar. He was full of excitement, yet apprehensive at the same time.

These contrasting emotions of delight and fright were at a peak on registration day. As he sat across the table from his faculty adviser, the professor asked him the big question, "What is your major?" The young man proudly responded, "Engineering." With that information, the two planned the freshman's schedule. It included the basic courses that all beginners take, but there were also a couple of professional courses in the field of engineering.

One of the subjects listed on the young man's schedule was chemistry. On the first day of class, the professor lectured while an assistant worked with a small glass test tube, a chemical, and a burner at a table on one side of the room.

Once the element in the test tube was heated, the assistant passed it along each row of seats in the classroom. The students were instructed to smell the burning substance. Suddenly, the room began to fill with the sounds of coughing, sneezing, and choking. When the young freshman passed the tube under his nose, he nearly lost his breath. To say the odor was similar to that of rotten eggs would be an understatement.

After the small glass tube finished its rounds, the professor announced that the students had been first-hand witnesses to burning sulfur. And the young student learned that what the Bible refers to as "brimstone" is today called sulfur. Knowing that sinners will spend eternity in a lake of burning brimstone (Revelation 19:20), the freshman entered a period of serious thought. Ultimately, his experiences that day contributed to his changing his major from engineering to the ministry.

A question of major concern for men is: "Where will you spend eternity?" After the Millennium will come the eternal state. Both saint and sinner will continue their existence in that world without end, but what awaits them differs radically. After pondering the subject, one should choose a final destiny with the righteous.

An Unforgettable Scene

When one looks at what the Bible says about the eternal state of the wicked, he discovers some sobering truths. Both Old and New Testaments discuss the matter.

Among the Old Testament writers who talk about the destiny of the unsaved dead is Isaiah. He contrasts the state of the righteous in the new heavens and the new earth with that of sinners (Isaiah 6:22-24). He says the faithful will periodically go to view the awful fate of the wicked. The carcasses of men who transgressed the law of God will lie in a place of corruption. Worms will eat their flesh. Fire will torture their bodies. Isaiah concludes: "They shall be an abhorring unto all flesh" (Isaiah 66:24).

Follow-up Discussion

As if to follow up the teachings of Isaiah, Jesus says the eternal state of the sinner will be "where their worm dieth not, and the fire is not quenched" (Mark 9:44). In the Greek, the name of the place is *gehenna*. As one of the words translated "hell" in the New Testament, it means literally "Valley of Hinnom."

The Valley of Hinnom ran alongside the southern edge of the city of Jerusalem. Among other things, it was once the site of heathen worship. Parents sacrificed their children on the altars to false gods erected in the area. During a time of revival, King Josiah ordered that the valley be defiled "that no man might make his son or daughter to pass through the fire to Molech" (2 Kings 23:10).

Defiling the sacred shrines of the god Molech probably included filling the valley with dead men's bones. The area then became the city dump. The carcasses of animals as well as the bodies of the poor were probably discarded there at times. Worms continuously worked on the decaying debris and the animal and human remains. Men kept the fires burning in an effort to control the filth of the dump.

When the Master said it would be better to amputate an offending hand, foot, or eye than to end up in that kind of hell, the audience got the message (Mark 9:42-48). They knew, of course, that He was speaking of *spiritual* surgery rather than mutilation of the body.

Prophesying in Parables

The New Testament contains other sobering words on the eternal state of the wicked. John the Baptist spoke of severe and eternal punishment for the sinner. Those whose lives bear wrong fruit will be cut down like trees and "cast into the fire" (Matthew 3:10). Like the chaff of wheat they will experience "unquenchable fire" (Matthew 3:12).

Jesus warned that uncontrolled anger might cause one to end up in "hell fire" (Matthew 5:22). Giving unbridled expression to the passion of lust will lead to the same end (Matthew 5:27-30). He even warned those whose religion was purely outward that a mere form of godliness will not guarantee heaven. To the most pious religious leaders of the day, the Master said: "Ye serpents, ye generation of vipers, how can ye escape the damnation of hell?" (Matthew 23:33).

Jesus also taught about the destiny of the wicked by parable. In the story of the marriage feast, He speaks of it as a place of "outer darkness" (Matthew 22:11-13). The uninvited guest at the feast is thrown out into the night. Deep darkness seems to be feared universally by men, but to show He is not simply talking of the darkness of the night, the Lord adds: "There shall be weeping and gnashing of teeth."

The same message comes through in the parable of the tares and wheat. The Master says that "in the end of this world," the two will be separated. The tares will then be cast into "a furnace of fire: there shall be wailing and gnashing of teeth" (Matthew 13:40-42).

This truth also appears in the parable of the unfaithful steward. He thought his master delayed his return from a trip, so he began to beat his fellow servants and to drink with the drunken. Jesus says the estate owner will come home unexpectedly. As to the fate of the steward, Jesus declares that he "shall cut him asunder, and appoint him his portion with the hypocrites: there shall be weeping and gnashing of teeth" (Matthew 24:43-51).

Again, in the story of the fish net, the Lord repeats His warning. When the net is pulled in, the good fish are kept, but the bad are cast away. Jesus says this illustrates what will happen at the end of the world. The angels will sever the wicked from the just and, according to the Master, "shall cast them into the furnace of fire: there shall be wailing and gnashing of teeth" (Matthew 13:47-50).

Outer darkness, weeping, and gnashing of teeth again appear as part of the eternal fate of the wicked in the Parable of the Talents (Matthew 25:14-30).

The Rich and the Poor

But among Jesus' most graphic descriptions of the sinner's destiny is the account of the rich man and Lazarus (Luke 16:19-31). After a brief story of the contrasting lives of the two men, the Lord tells of their deaths. Upon leaving this world, the poor man went to "Abraham's bosom." The rich man "died, and was buried." Jesus adds, "And in hell he lifted up his eyes."

The remainder of the story shows what hell is like. It is a place of fire. The rich man complained, "I am tormented in this flame." Death by burning seems among the worst types of death in this world. But what of an eternity of it?

Hell is a place not only of extreme suffering, but also of unsatisfied desire. The rich man asked for water to cool his tongue and was denied. Hell is also a place of memory and remorse. Abraham said to the rich man, "Son, remember . . . ." He not only remembered how he had mistreated the poor man Lazarus, but he also recalled the lost condition of his five brothers who were yet alive and wished he could do something about it now.

Finally, the account of the rich man and Lazarus shows the eternal state of the wicked to be one of hopelessness. Abraham told the rich man the gulf between him and Lazarus could never be crossed. Hope gives courage to face impossible circumstances in this life. But what of the day when all hope for the sinner is gone?

Visions of Hell

John's writings also give insight into the destiny of evil men. Among the many things revealed to the apostle were visions of men in hell. John gives solemn warning that men must cease living lives of sin. In a plea that they do not follow the Antichrist he writes:

The same shall drink of the wine of the wrath of God, which is poured out without mixture into the cup of his indignation; and he shall be tormented with fire and brimstone in the presence of the holy angels, and in the presence of the Lamb: and the smoke of their torment ascendeth up for ever and ever: and they have no rest day nor night (Revelation 14:10,11).

No wonder the apostle speaks of the destiny of the wicked as the "second death" (Revelation 21:8). They will simply die eternally!

But John's visions of men in hell are probably the grimmest when they show that the suffering of sinners in eternity will include the pain of separation from God and all that is good. For example, he states that the wicked will be shut out of the Holy City forever:

> And there shall in no wise enter into it any thing that defileth, neither whatsoever worketh abomination, or maketh a lie....For without are dogs, and sorcerers, and whoremongers, and murderers, and idolators, and whosoever loveth and maketh a lie (Revelation 21:27; 22:15).

No Second Chance

None of these passages concerning the eternal state of the wicked agree with teachings such as universalism. This false doctrine says punishment for sin will be temporary. By and by all will be restored to God, even Satan and the fallen angels. But John says the devil will be "tormented day and night for ever and ever" (Revelation 20:10).

It does little good for men to reason that God is love and therefore will not condemn men to hell eternally. God is also just, and His law demands an awful penalty for sin. It must be paid, one way or another. Jesus provided the way of love if men will accept it.

125

Nor does it help when others cry, "But God is the Father of all men. He would never punish His children in hell." Jesus said the devil is the spiritual father of sinners (John 8:44).

To reason that suffering temporarily in hell will change men so that God can restore them to favor is to suggest that its fires can accomplish what God's grace failed to do. Universalism is a doctrine without a Biblical basis.

Annihilationism is another false view of the eternal state of the wicked. It says one of two things. One position simply suggests that at death all ends for the sinner. But, rather than a cessation of existence, the Bible teaches a change in the condition of existence at death. The other teaching of annihilationism is that the sinner will finally be rescued from hell by being totally destroyed. But this would amount to a double penalty for sin. Not even the laws of man permit such. The Bible contains the truth about the destiny of evil men— eternal punishment in the lake of fire.

By Way of Contrast

As to the eternal state of the righteous, Scripture shows it will be as wonderful as the state of the sinner will be awful. This contrast appears in the story of the judgment in Matthew's Gospel. Those who are judged evil will "go away into everlasting punishment: but the righteous into life eternal" (Matthew 25:46). To the one, the Judge says, "Depart from me, ye cursed, into everlasting fire," but to the other, "Come, ye blessed of my Father, inherit the kingdom prepared for you from the foundation of the world" (Matthew 25:34,41).

Moreover, in His parables, Jesus illustrates the radically different experiences of the saint and sinner in eternity. After telling of the banishment of the wicked to an eternity of fire and weeping, He says: "Then shall the righteous shine forth as the sun in the kingdom of their Father" (Matthew 13:43).

A Heavenly Home

According to the details Scripture provides, much of what was discussed in the preceding chapter concerning the condition of the righteous during their intermediate state will simply continue into their eternal state. The difference is that their somewhat limited blessings will come into fullness during eternity. The Bible speaks of the perfection of experience that awaits them after the resurrection (Hebrews 11:40).

Scripture uses various expressions to convey the wonders of the eternal heavenly home of the righteous. Paradise is one of these. This term reminds one of the Garden, and promises a return to the perfect conditions of Adam and Eve in Eden.

Heaven is also viewed, for the Christian, as the Father's house. This brings to mind the idea of a home, security, and fellowship. The end of the believer's journey is called a heavenly country. This suggests rest for the weary traveler. The believer also expects to find a city when he reaches his destination. It is said of Abraham: "He looked for a city which hath foundations, whose builder and maker is God" (Hebrews 11:10). Perhaps the idea suggested here is that of an organized and peaceful society.

But more than anything, while the sinner is eternally separated from God, the saint will be with Him forevermore (Revelation 21:3). The Lord will be so manifestly present everywhere in the city that there will be no need for sacred places there. John declares: "I saw no temple therein: for the Lord God Almighty and the Lamb are the temple of it" (Revelation 21:22).

Determined Destinies

The time will come when the eternal destinies of men will be permanently determined. At that time, John's words will apply:

> He that is unjust, let him be unjust still: and he which is filthy, let him be filthy still: and he that is righteous, let him be righteous still: and he that is holy, let him be holy still (Revelation 22:11).

But in the meantime, John has a better word for all who will listen. He writes:

> And the Spirit and the bride say, Come. And let him that heareth say, Come. And let him that is athirst come. And whosoever will, let him take the water of life freely (Revelation 22:17).

There are two ways to travel on earth. One way leads to destruction and the other to life. The future belongs to those who find life in Jesus.